DATE DUE

FE 19 '93			
MR 25 '94			
JE 17 '94			
DE 9 '94			
MR 3 '95			
MR 24 '95			
RENEW			
AP 8 '96			
FE 96			
JY 8 '97			
NO 24 '97			
SE 11 '98			
MR 10 '99			

NORTHERN IRELAND

NORTHERN IRELAND

MICHAEL
KRONENWETTER

FRANKLIN WATTS
NEW YORK / LONDON / TORONTO / SYDNEY
1990

Photographs courtesy of: Reuters/Bettmann: pp. 15, 103, 107; Wide World
Photos: pp. 19, 64 top; The Bettmann Archive: pp. 31, 42, 49, 50, 55;
UPI/Bettmann: pp. 59, 67, 113, 119, 136; Magnum Photos: pp. 64 bottom
(Chris Steele-Perkins), 75 (Stuart Franklin); Impact Visuals: pp. 82 (Maggie
Miller), 85, 87, 89, 100 (all Donna DeCesare), 110 (Peter C. Jones),
120 (Jim West).

Library of Congress Cataloging-in-Publication Data

Kronenwetter, Michael.
Northern Ireland / by Michael Kronenwetter.
p.   cm.
Includes bibliographical references.
Summary: An examination of the religious and political tensions
existing in Northern Ireland, from their historical origins to
present-day conflicts, and looks at efforts to bring peace to this
region.
ISBN 0-531-10942-9
1. Northern Ireland—Juvenile literature.   [1. Northern Ireland.]
I. Title.
DA990.U46K77   1990
941.6—dc20   90-33571   CIP   AC

CONTENTS

NORTHERN IRELAND

North Channel

DONEGAL

LONDON-
DERRY

ANTRIM

NORTHERN
IRELAND

TYRONE

Belfast • • Newtownards

DOWN

LEIT-
RIM

FERM-
ANAGH

ARMAGH

SLIGO

MONA-
GHAN

MAYO

ROS-
COMMON

CAVAN

LOUTH

LONG-
FORD

GALWAY

WEST-
MEATH

MEATH

OFFALY

DUBLIN

KIL-
DARE

• Dublin

IRELAND

LAOIGHIS

WICKLOW

CLAIRE

CARL-
OW

TIPPER-
ARY

• Limerick

KIL-
KENNY

LIMERICK

WEX-
FORD

KERRY

CORK

Waterford •

WATERFORD

Cork •

St. George's Channel

0   50 Miles

1

ULSTER

Northern Ireland is an unusual and troubled land.

Technically, together with England, Scotland, and Wales, it is a province of the United Kingdom. "Legally," as the author Richard Rose has written, Northern Ireland "is a subordinate part of the United Kingdom. Historically, it is an insubordinate part."[1]

The *Encyclopaedia Britannica* describes it as a "self-governing state within the United Kingdom."[2] But, in reality, it has not governed itself for almost two decades. For all that time, it has been ruled from London, England, and not from its own capital city of Belfast. Even today, it remains one of the few places on earth with no government of its own.

Located on the northeastern corner of the island of Ireland, Northern Ireland was cut off from the rest of Ireland in 1921. It was made up of six of the nine counties that once formed the ancient Irish province of Ulster. People often refer to Northern Ireland as Ulster even now.

Northern Ireland is a small place. It is only 110 miles across at its widest point, and only 85 miles from north to south. With an area of about 5,452 square miles, it is roughly one-fifth the size of the Republic of Ireland, with which it shares not only an island but most of its history. Its entire population is a little over one and one-half million, about the same as the Kansas City metropolitan area.[3]

Despite its small size, Ulster gets more than its share of attention—particularly from the United States. American interest in Irish affairs is not surprising. According to the U.S. Census Bureau, over 43,752,000 Americans have Irish ancestors.[4] That's over eight times the current population of Northern Ireland and the Republic of Ireland put together!

THE TROUBLES

Sadly, most of the world's interest in Ulster is centered on the bitter struggle that has been raging over the future of the province, ever since it was set off from the rest of Ireland seven decades ago.

There are four main parties to that struggle: two are political forces within Ulster itself, and two are outside governments. The two internal forces are the unionists (sometimes known as the loyalists) and the nationalists. The unionists, almost all of whom are Protestants, make up about two-thirds of Ulster's population. They are determined to keep Ulster within the United Kingdom. The nationalists, almost all of whom are Roman Catholics, are just as determined to reunite Ulster with the rest of Ireland.

The two outside governments with a stake in Ulster's future are, of course, the United Kingdom and the Republic of Ireland. The United Kingdom (or U.K.) is dominated by England, the country that controlled all of Ireland as a kind of colony until 1921. For its part, the Republic of Ireland has never fully accepted the partition (or division) of Ireland that took place in that year.

Between them, these four forces have turned tiny Ulster into one of the world's hotspots of the political violence known as terrorism. (For more about the nature of Irish terrorism, see Chapter 7.) Although such statistics are not kept for every country, Ulster probably has the highest per capita rate of terrorism in the world. In the twenty years from 1969 to 1988, 2,690 people were killed in the political violence there.[5] That would be the equivalent of over 405,000 deaths in the United States.

The Irish have a word for this outpouring of bloodshed. They call it the Troubles. It seems like too small a word to sum up so much anger, sorrow, and pain. Riots, bombings, stabbings, and even machine-gunnings have become almost daily occurrences in Northern Ireland. It is a rare week that goes by without at least one killing related to the Troubles. In some weeks, there are many more.

Most of these deaths get little attention outside of Northern Ireland itself. But, every now and then, the ongoing violence erupts in some new and tragic way that thrusts Northern Ireland into the very center of world attention.

This is what happened in July 1972, when a series of bombs set off by a terrorist group known as the Provisional (Provo) Wing of the Irish Republican Army killed thirteen people and wounded ten times that many in Belfast. It happened again in August 1979, when another Provo bomb blew up on a yacht belonging to the British war hero Earl Louis Mountbatten, killing both him and his fourteen-year-old grandson. It happened again in 1984, when still another bomb destroyed the hotel room of British prime minister, Margaret Thatcher, in the English resort town of Brighton. She was not there at the time.

And, most horribly of all, it happened in March 1988. Within only a few days of that month, three of the parties to the struggle demonstrated, one after the other, just how sudden, how ruthless, and how deadly they could be.

THREE DEATHS IN GIBRALTAR

The first link in the chain of death was forged almost 1,300 miles from Ulster, on a high peninsula off the coast of Spain. Although it is connected to Spain by a narrow strip of land, the Rock of Gibraltar has been claimed by Great Britain since 1704. Only 2¾ miles long, and about ¾ of a mile wide, Gibraltar is a tourist center. It is also the home of the Barbary ape, the only monkey native to Europe, and the site of an important British naval base.

Visitors who passed the three people strolling down a quiet Gibraltar street that day in March might have guessed that they were fellow tourists. The pretty young woman and her two male companions were all dressed in light, casual clothes, the kind tourists wear sightseeing in the warm weather of Gibraltar in the spring.

But Mairead Farrell, Sean Savage, and Daniel McCann were not tourists. They were terrorists. They were members of one of the most feared terrorist organizations in the entire world—the Provos. Claiming to represent the oppressed Catholic minority of Northern Ireland, the Provos have sworn to drive the British out of their country.

According to the British government, the three terrorists had come to Gibraltar to kill British soldiers. They were planning to set off a car bomb that they hoped would explode in the midst of a British army band.[6] If so, they never got the chance. Within seconds, they were dead, gunned down in the street by members of a British army antiterrorist unit known as the Special Air Service (or SAS).

There is evidence that Farrell, Savage, and Mc-Cann were deliberately killed—or executed—by the SAS. According to Larry Cox, of the respected London-based human rights group Amnesty International, there are "eyewitness reports that [they] were not given a fair warning," and "that [they] were shot after they were on the ground."[7]

There was other evidence as well. None of the three was carrying any kind of weapon when they were killed. The physical evidence suggests that they were approached, and shot, from behind. Mairead Farrell, for example, was shot at least five times. Two of the bullets entered her head. Three were in her back.[8] Despite all this, a jury in a British court in Gibraltar ruled that the killings had been "lawful."[9]

News of the killings was met with horror and outrage by many of the Catholics of Northern Ireland. But the horror and outrage were just beginning. The chain of death that had begun in Gibraltar would soon stretch all the way to Northern Ireland.

TWO FUNERALS IN BELFAST

The three terrorists were to be buried in Milltown Cemetery, in the Andersonstown area of Belfast, the capital of Northern Ireland. Andersonstown is a heavily

Catholic neighborhood and a major stronghold of the Irish Republican Army—the IRA.

The IRA keeps a special section of Milltown Cemetery marked off by a green picket fence. It is there that it buries its honored heroes. It was there that a single grave was dug for the three victims of the SAS.[10]

The quiet and dignified ceremony was conducted with a sense of military ritual. Black gloves and black berets—the traditional symbols of IRA activists killed in the line of duty—were placed on top of the coffins as they were carried to the grave. There was even a large color guard. Some carried black flags, others IRA flags, and still others the red, white, and green flags of the Irish Republic.

Funerals are very important to the IRA. It is estimated that between five thousand and ten thousand people were gathered in the cemetery that day.[11] Some of them were journalists. Some, no doubt, were undercover police. But most were members or supporters of the IRA, who had come to mourn the dead terrorists they thought of as martyred heroes. Several of them had brought their children along, passing on an old family tradition of attending IRA funerals. The large crowd kept a respectful silence as it made its way slowly to the grave. The color guard lined up at the graveside as a priest led the prayers.

At the last minute, the gloves and berets were taken from the coffins and handed to the closest relatives of the dead IRA members. Then, the first of the coffins was lowered down. Then the second . . .

Suddenly, without warning, the silence was shattered by a loud explosion. More explosions followed, punctuated by the slap of pistol shots. People began to fall, dead or wounded, onto the ground. Some of the

Above: Hearses carrying the coffins of shot IRA guerrillas Sean Savage, Danny McCann, and Mairead Farrell move to the Milltown Cemetery, followed by several thousand mourners. Left: Mourners at the cemetery take cover when a gunman shot at the crowd. The man turned out to be a vehement anti-Catholic Protestant.

crowd began to run. Some ducked for cover behind tombstones. Some turned in search of their attackers.

There was only one—a bearded man in dark clothes with a flat cap on his head and a belt of hand grenades around his waist. He was standing a little way back from the mourners, lobbing hand grenade after hand grenade into the crowd.

A television camera on the opposite side of the crowd recorded the eerie scene as the attacker began to retreat. From so far away, things seemed to be happening almost in slow motion, as the man backed away through the gravestones, firing his pistol at those members of the crowd who dared to chase after him.

The attacker made his way past the rows of graves and began to move up an incline, heavy with tall grass and weeds, toward a highway in the distance. As he went, he tossed still more grenades. Their force spewed dirt and rocks a hundred feet into the air.

But his pursuers kept coming. They were unorganized but relentless, spread out across the hillside like a rolling wave. And finally, before he could reach the highway, the wave closed in over him. As the enraged crowd attacked the attacker, police from the Royal Ulster Constabulary moved in and arrested him.

The man turned out to be a fanatically anti-Catholic Protestant named Michael Stone. He did not seem to care what happened to him. All he wanted was to know how many Catholics he had killed. Amazingly—considering the size of the crowd and the number of grenades he had thrown—the answer was only three. Sixty more were injured. [12]

One of the dead was a twenty-one-year-old man named Kevin Brady. Brady's own funeral would provide the final link in this particular chain of violence in Ulster. It took place just three days later, on March 19.

Tensions were high in Belfast that day, as the funeral procession left the church and made its way toward the cemetery.

Brady had been a taxi driver, and the procession was made up largely of the black taxicabs that are a familiar sight in the British Isles. The big black vehicles moved slowly and solemnly through a narrow Belfast street, surrounded by a large crowd of mourners on foot. Another Ulster martyr was being taken to his grave. [13]

Then, as if from nowhere, a small silver car came swinging around a corner, only to find itself blocked by the funeral procession. The car slammed to a halt. The two young men in the front seat of the car at first looked confused, then terrified. They had good reason to be frightened.

Although they were dressed in civilian clothes, the two men were, in fact, off-duty members of the British army—the hated enemy of the IRA. They had gotten lost and had somehow stumbled onto the route of the funeral procession by mistake.

The driver put the car in gear and drove up onto the sidewalk, starting a U-turn he hoped would allow him to turn the car around and speed away. But there was little room to maneuver because of the crowd.

As the car jerked into reverse, the passenger stuck his head and upper body out of the side window and waved an automatic pistol at the crowd to frighten them. He even fired it into the air.

The driver jammed the car into first gear, and the car lurched forward. But, just then, one of the massive black taxis pulled up in front of the car and braked there. The little car was trapped.

In a few sickeningly short seconds, the solemn crowd had become a mob. It surged forward. The two men—whose names were Derek Woods and David Howes—were pulled from the car. The one with the gun made no attempt to fire it into the crowd, even as they were being dragged from the car and viciously beaten, their clothes half torn off in the process.

Provos appeared from the crowd and took charge, shoving the battered men into one of the taxis. Now, the crowd made way, as the taxi containing the IRA men and the soldiers pulled off.

It didn't go far. Apparently unaware that a helicopter had followed them from the funeral and was watching from above, the Provos drove the car into an apparently hidden alleyway. Videotapes taken from the helicopter show that the two soldiers were pulled from the car, Woods collapsing to the ground. A Provo standing over him shot him through the head. Howes crouched down beside the taxi, his arms thrown over his head. He, too, was shot dead.[14]

HOW CAN THESE THINGS HAPPEN?

The events of March 1988 shocked people around the world. But they did not really shock the people of Ulster. They are accustomed to events like these. Father Alex Reid happened to be present at both disrupted funerals. He even tried to give "the kiss of life" to one of the dying British soldiers. Asked about it later, he said there was nothing unusual about what had happened. He'd often given the Last Sacrament to victims of the Troubles. "The only extraordinary thing," he said, "was that there were photographers nearby, so everybody saw."[15]

The television pictures were particularly powerful. They brought the terrible events in Belfast home to

*On the same day as the IRA members' funeral,
two British soldiers were attacked and killed
as their car apparently made a wrong turn and
the men became tangled up with the funeral.*

people throughout the developed world, who watched in horror as Michael Stone was shown tossing hand grenades into the crowd at Milltown Cemetery and saw the mob dragging the two young British soldiers out of their car to certain death.

The scenes were particularly shocking to many Americans, whose families had come from Ireland or Great Britain. How could these things happen? they asked themselves. How could British government officials gun down unarmed people on a public street? How could an Irishman throw hand grenades into a crowd of mourners at a funeral? How could still another group of mourners, at still another funeral, brutally beat, and then murder, two young men for the terrible crime of getting lost in the streets of Belfast?

And beyond those questions were the others. What are the Troubles in Northern Ireland really about? How did they begin, and why? And when—if ever— will they end?

2

ENGLAND IN IRELAND—EIGHT HUNDRED YEARS OF CONFLICT

In order to understand a country's present, it is useful to know about its past. In order to understand Northern Ireland, it is absolutely vital to know something about the eight hundred years of English presence on the island of Ireland.

The past and the present are so entangled in Northern Ireland that it is often impossible to tell them apart. Events that took place centuries ago still affect the way people think and feel and act today.

Many of the people of Northern Ireland are still reacting against injustices and oppressions that took place hundreds of years before they were born. They talk about events that happened two hundred, three hundred, or even eight hundred years ago as if they had happened yesterday—and happened to them personally. Most of those events have to do with Ireland's relationship to England, a relationship that has been marred by bitterness, violence, and cruelty.

Militants on both sides of the current struggle in Ulster feel that they are continuing a battle that began centuries ago. They see themselves as seeking to avenge old wrongs, carrying on the cause of fallen heroes, and fighting against villains who have been dead for centuries.

What follows is a brief outline of the tangled history of Ulster—a history that is inseparable from the history of the rest of Ireland. Without understanding it, it is impossible to understand what is happening in Northern Ireland today.

THE CELTS— THE ORIGINAL IRISH

For over a thousand years before the birth of Christ, tribes of people called Celts dominated most of Europe. Celtic tribes conquered much of the mighty Roman Empire, plundering Rome itself in the fourth century B.C. They eventually came to settle largely in the British Isles—first in England and Scotland, and finally, on the island of Ireland as well.

Ireland, in fact, was invaded by several different Celtic tribes in turn, over the course of more than a thousand years. The last of the invading tribes, known as the Gaels, probably crossed the Irish Sea from England around the time of Christ. [1]

Once in Ireland, the Celts remained divided into tribes, each of which was ruled by its own king. These tribes often warred among themselves. It seems the tradition of Irishmen fighting each other goes back a long, long way. On the other hand, the tribes shared a common language (Gaelic) and had many friendly dealings with each other. Some tribes even joined in loose unions under strong chieftains who would then take the title of High Kings. One of the most important of the ancient Irish kingdoms—which at one time occupied most of the northern part of Ireland—was known as Ulaid, or Ulster.

The Celts had their own religion, which they practiced for centuries in Ireland. But many of the Celts in Ireland were converted to Christianity in the fifth century A.D. Credit for this is usually given to Saint Patrick, a British churchman who was the second bishop of Ireland.

Like many other figures in Irish history, Patrick is surrounded with myth. One story claims that he was a slave in Ireland long before he became a bishop there. Another says that he drove all the snakes out of Ireland and that he made the green shamrock a symbol of Ireland by using it so often as the symbol of the Holy Trinity.

In any case, Patrick was a Roman Catholic, and from the fifth century on, Ireland as a whole has been primarily a Roman Catholic nation. What is more, Patrick worked particularly hard in the north of Ireland. From his time on, the Catholics of the north have had the reputation of being the most devout of all the Irish.

THE ENGLISH ARRIVE

Although Ireland remained Celtic, England did not. It was invaded first by the Saxons, from what is now Germany, and later by the Normans, from Normandy in western France. By the time Britain came to dominate Ireland, its culture was very different from that of Ireland. It had been much more influenced by the Saxon and Norman cultures than by that of the Celts.

In 1169, an English lord of Norman descent named Richard Strongbow sailed across the Irish Sea with a boatload of his men. He had been invited to Ireland by a tribal king named Dermot MacMurrough of Leinster.

The king wanted Strongbow's help in a power struggle he was having with one of the High Kings.[2]

Strongbow married a Celtic princess and stayed in Ireland. Other Norman lords soon followed him from England, taking lands and building castles for themselves on the island. All this activity caused King Henry II of England to launch an invasion of Ireland in 1171, to make sure that the Norman barons stayed loyal to the English Crown. From that time on, England has claimed a role in the affairs of Ireland.

It was a troubled role from the beginning. As one nineteenth-century history book explained: "Ireland had been conquered by Henry II . . . and the country was henceforward under English rule, but in a state of disorder. For [the next] hundred years it was the constant scene of battling between the Irish chiefs and the English invaders and their descendants."[3]

During much of that three hundred years, the English Crown had little real control over what happened in most of Ireland. The Crown could hold the walled towns, like Dublin, the largest city in Ireland, but it could not control the countryside.

It was said that British power really reached only to the edge of the Pale, an area about 20 miles wide around Dublin. All the rest of Ireland was "beyond the Pale"—a wild country outside of English control. In the countryside, the Irish nobles and the Old English (the descendants of the Normans) did whatever they wanted. They lived by Irish law, or by no law at all. They fought among themselves, or joined together, as they pleased, happily ignoring the wishes of the English Crown.

Britain made several efforts to assert its authority, but most of them were ineffective. Even many of the English lords who were sent to Ireland to assert British control "went native." It was said that they became *Hibernicis ipsis hiberniores*—"more Irish than the Irish themselves."[4] In 1366, the Crown issued the Statutes of Kilkenny, which ordered the Old English to stop behaving like Irishmen and to start obeying English, rather than Irish, laws. But those statutes could not be enforced.

ENGLAND TAKES CONTROL

In 1534, King Henry VIII of England renounced (or broke) England's bonds with the Catholic church in Rome. He declared himself the head of the Christian Church in all of Great Britain, which included the English domains in Ireland. What has become known as the Church of England, or the Anglican Church, was made the official religion of Ireland.

But Ireland had been Catholic for over one thousand years, and the faith of many Irish Catholics ran deep. They considered the Pope the leader of the Christian church everywhere on earth, and they were not about to recognize the British monarch as head of the church in Ireland.

In the same year, Henry declared that as king of Ireland he was claiming his right to all the land in Ireland. He could then hand it out again, to whomever he saw fit. This right gave the king an extremely powerful weapon with which to punish unfaithful nobles (by not returning their lands), or to reward faithful ones (by regranting the lands to them).

Henry did little more than claim this right. But his daughter, Queen Elizabeth I, actually sent English troops to Ireland to enforce it. Not surprisingly, the Gaels resented the British troops. Many, although far from all, rebelled. During Elizabeth's long reign

(1558–1603), she had to put down six separate Irish rebellions.[5] At least two of them—including the last and bloodiest of them all—began in Ulster.[6]

In 1603, Queen Elizabeth died and was followed on both the English and the Irish thrones by King James I. That same year, the leader of the last rebellion, the earl of Tyrone, was finally forced to submit to English rule. He and another ex-rebel leader left Ireland on September 14, 1607, an event that is known in Irish history as "the Flight of the Earls."

Even before that, the queen had taken steps to end any threat of future rebellions in Ireland. English troops were stationed throughout the country, to see to it that English law would be enforced. Even worse, from the point of view of the Irish Catholics, Protestantism was proclaimed the official religion of Ireland.[7]

PROTESTANT SETTLEMENTS
IN ULSTER

James I tried to ensure loyalty in Ulster by populating the region with Protestant settlers loyal to Britain. Lands were taken from the Catholic lords in Ulster and transferred to new immigrants from England and Scotland.

About thirteen thousand of these colonizers were already settled on plantations in Ireland by 1622. These first arrivals were almost equally divided between English and Scots. Over the next few decades, however, most of the new settlers would come across the narrow channel from Scotland. Almost all of the Scots were Presbyterian Protestants, in contrast to the English settlers, who were Anglicans of the Church of England. Eventually, most of their descendants would become members of the Church of Ireland, the Irish branch of the Church of England.

The English and Scottish immigrants settled in various areas throughout Ireland. But it was only in Ulster—directly across from Scotland—that they came to form the majority of the population.

The British monarch had hoped they would be more than a majority. The Crown's hope was that the colonizers would drive the native Irish out altogether, replacing them with British tenants who were loyal to the British king. But the newcomers realized that they could make more profit for themselves by running their plantations with Irish labor. They kept many of the inhabitants—most of whom were Catholics—to work their fields. [8]

There was tension and hostility among all these groups. The Old English were usually Catholic, but they were also Royalist. They still felt some loyalty to the British Crown. The Gaelic Irish, on the other hand, were anti-Royalist, and longed for the right of the Irish to rule themselves. But the Old English and the Gaelic Irish both considered the new Scottish and English settlers as interlopers who had come to take their lands. Many of those new arrivals, in turn, thought of *all* native Irish men and women, the Old English and the Gaels alike, as barbarians.

At the same time, many of the Irish and the Scots, new and old, felt a strong personal dislike for the English. Many of the English, meanwhile, were not fond of either of them. And each of the major religious groups—Catholics, Anglicans, and Presbyterians—thought of the others as heretics. Their religions unfortunately taught that all other religions were wrong, if not positively evil.

The patterns of settlement made by the English Anglicans and the Scottish Presbyterians among the Gaelic Irish and Old English Catholics are still reflected in Northern Ireland's population today.[9] So are the tensions that existed between them.

In 1641, many of the Gaelic and Old English Catholics joined forces against the new settlers. In taking up arms, however, they were not rebelling against English rule in Ireland. They just wanted their lands back. Once again, the heart of the rebellion was in Ulster.

The uprising was exceptionally brutal. In Portadown, for instance, the mostly Catholic rebels threw scores of Protestant men, women, and children off a bridge. Some of them drowned. Others were beaten to death by the oars of Irishmen in boats as they swam for safety. Still others were shot or clubbed to death as they dragged themselves ashore. A Portadown resident later testified that many Protestants in the town were tortured, stabbed, whipped, and left "wallowing in their blood to languish and starve . . . to death."[10]

The Protestants responded with several outrages of their own. But the worst of the violence was yet to come. In 1649, English armies led by the Puritan Oliver Cromwell arrived in Ireland. They put down the rebellion with merciless efficiency. Even after one large group of rebels had surrendered, Cromwell reported that "their officers were knocked on the head, and every tenth man of the soldiers killed." The rest were sent as virtual slaves to the distant Caribbean. It was, in Cromwell's view, "the righteous judgment of God upon these barbarous wretches."[11]

By 1653, Cromwell had brought all of Ireland under English control. The remaining lands of the Irish rebels had been taken from them and given to Protestants—many brought over from England or

Scotland to claim them—or to the few native Gaelic leaders who had refused to take part in the rebellion. [12]

The hopes of the Catholics in Ireland rose briefly in 1685, when a Catholic monarch, James II, became king of England, Scotland, and Ireland. But James II was deposed in 1688, and his throne was taken by his Protestant son-in-law, William of Orange. James escaped to Ireland, where he tried to raise an army to take back the throne. Many Irish Catholics flocked to his cause. King William, however, led his own army to Ireland and quickly defeated James's largely Irish troops. The anniversary of one battle in that campaign, the Battle of the Boyne, is still celebrated by Ulster's Protestants as a symbol of their dominance over the Catholics. The actual surrender came at Limerick in 1691.

William's victory over James ended all chance for Catholic control in Ireland for the next three centuries. To this day, James's defeat is still bitterly regretted in the Catholic households of Ulster, and admiring portraits of King William are still hung in Protestant homes. Many powerful Ulster Protestants belong to the Orange Order, named for William of Orange, which celebrates the "Protestant ascendancy" in Ulster. [13]

THE PENAL LAWS

For most of the next three hundred years, England remained the dominant force not only in Ulster but in the rest of Ireland as well. The Irish parliament at Dublin was controlled by Protestants, but even it could do little that the government in England did not approve.

Within a few years of James's defeat, it became clear that the Irish Catholics were in for a hard time. A series of harsh laws, called the Penal Laws, were passed to punish Catholics for opposing the Protestant monarchs of England. The laws virtually eliminated the civil rights of all Irishmen who did not belong to the Church of Ireland.

The Penal Laws began by severely restricting the rights of Catholics to practice their religion. But they went far beyond religious matters. Catholics were not allowed to hold public office—on the grounds that the oath of office was a Protestant oath that Catholics could not swear to. (But they were not allowed to vote either, and no oath was required to vote.) In addition, Catholics were forbidden to carry firearms, or even to own any kind of military weapon.

Their economic rights were almost as harshly restricted as their political and religious rights. Their right to own land was severely limited, and they were even forbidden to own a horse worth more than five pounds.

Although the Penal Laws never succeeded in destroying the Catholic religion in Ireland, they were very effective in destroying Catholic economic power. By 1714, Catholics owned only 7 percent of the land, [14] most of it being the poorest land in the country. [15]

For a long time, Catholics could not even rent the lands they had once owned. The best they could do for themselves was to hire out as farm laborers, at pathetic wages, to the poor Protestant tenants of wealthy Anglo-Irish landowners. ("Anglo-Irish" refers to the Irish of English descent.)

Catholic children were forbidden to attend school. Catholic parents countered by organizing "hedge schools," teaching their children as best they could in secret places in the woods, or behind hedges. But the effect of the ban was to keep most Catholics as ignorant as they were poor.

IRELAND NEVER WAS SO QUIET AS IT IS NOW. —*Cable Dispatch*.

Things were not very good for poor Protestants, either, particularly for those of the Presbyterian faith. The Penal Laws applied to dissenting Protestants (non-Anglicans) as well as to Catholics.[16] While most Presbyterians probably managed to stay a step above their Catholic neighbors, it was often a very small step.

In many ways, then, the Catholics and Presbyterians were natural allies against their Anglo-Irish neighbors and Ireland's English masters. Real power over all of Ireland was in the hands of the English, while local wealth and authority were firmly in the hands of the Irish who belonged to the Church of Ireland.

Even some of the Anglo-Irish resented England's power. The great Anglican writer and churchman, Jonathan Swift, was extremely hostile to both Catholics and Presbyterians. But he was also intensely bitter against the English. He once suggested that the Irish should burn everything English except their coal.[17]

THE PATRIOTS

A group of Protestant members of the Irish parliament known as the "Patriots" won a so-called declaration of independence from the English Crown in 1782. Symbolically, at least, this was a major step for Ireland. It meant that most of the laws affecting Ireland would now be made by the Parliament in Dublin, not by the one at Westminster in London.

But in reality it made little difference. Westminster still had the right to veto any action of the Irish parliament it didn't like. And Westminster kept the power to grant government jobs in Ireland as well.

This limited independence also did little to change the balance of power among the Irish themselves. The

Anglo-Irish kept their control over the Irish parliament, thanks largely to the fact that Catholics still could not vote.

The Patriots, led by Henry Grattan, wanted this to change. They worked for Catholic emancipation, which would allow Catholics not only to vote but to sit in Parliament as well. In 1793, they were partly successful. The Catholic Relief Act was passed, giving Catholics the first right, although not the second.[18] That would not be won for over thirty years, when a Catholic named Daniel O'Connell would actually take a seat in the British Parliament at Westminster. In the meantime, England's rule in Ireland was threatened by a movement led not by a Catholic but by a Protestant.

THE UNITED IRISHMEN AND THE DREAM OF AN IRISH REPUBLIC

In 1791, a young Presbyterian lawyer named Wolfe Tone founded the United Irish Society at Belfast. Tone was rebellious by nature. He had spent a lot of time in France in the midst of the French Revolution, and he was vividly aware that the American colonies had thrown off English rule only a few years before.

The constitution of the United Irishmen declared that Ireland was "ruled by Englishmen and the Servants of Englishmen, whose Object is the Interest of another Country, whose instrument is Corruption, and Whose Strength is the Weakness of Ireland. . . ."[19]

The solution, as Wolfe Tone saw it, was for all Irishmen to join together against England. He wanted his countrymen to stop thinking of themselves—and each other—as Protestants or Catholics, and to start thinking of themselves as Irishmen instead.

Tone's United Irishmen was not openly revolutionary, at least not at first. Its constitution called only for "a complete and radical Reform of the Representation of the People in Parliament" so that it would include "Irishmen of every religious Persuasion."[20]

It was at least partly pressure from the United Irishmen that forced the British Parliament to try to calm the situation in Ireland by passing the Catholic Relief Act in 1793. But the Catholic Relief Act did not satisfy Tone. As time went on, support for the United Irishmen grew, and that organization edged closer and closer to outright rebellion.

Tone's ideas appealed largely to two groups. One was the young Presbyterian revolutionaries in Ulster, who were inspired by the talk of "liberty, equality, and fraternity" that was coming out of France. The other group was made up of the peasant and middle-class Catholics in the rural areas of southern Ireland, who saw the movement as a way of getting back their rights, and perhaps even their long-lost lands.

For a time, it seemed as though Tone's effort to unite Presbyterians and Catholics might succeed. Soon after he founded the Belfast branch of the United Irishmen, which was made up largely of Presbyterians, he and a Catholic leader named James Napper Tandy formed a second branch in the heavily Catholic south. Tone himself was even elected secretary of a Catholic organization (the Catholic Committee) in Dublin.[21]

Tone went to France for help in freeing Ireland from British rule. The revolutionary government of France was no friend of any monarchy, much less the British one. In 1796, a fleet of thirty-five French ships set sail for Ireland, with thousands of French troops on board. The invasion might have succeeded. There were fewer than five hundred government defenders on shore to meet it when the fleet arrived at Bantry

Bay, on the southwest edge of Ireland, on December 21, 1796. But the defenders had a powerful ally in the December weather. A terrific gale blew up off the ocean. The tearing winds and rolling seas prevented the ships from landing, and finally drove them out of the bay altogether. The advantage of surprise was lost, and the French ships set sail for home.

The British responded to the failed invasion by cracking down on the rebels in Ireland. This crackdown began in Ulster. Torture was used, widely and without mercy, to force suspected rebels to turn informer. Many did. In the end, thousands of people were arrested, and the United Irishmen were all but destroyed.

Nonetheless, Tone and his remaining allies never entirely gave up hope. A haphazard rebellion broke out in 1798, this time in County Wexford in the Catholic south. As in earlier uprisings, there were reports—some of them true—of atrocities on both sides.

The Protestant-led militia had been terrorizing and sometimes torturing the Catholic peasantry in Wexford ever since the failed rebellion of 1796. The Wexford uprising itself was inspired by a massacre of prisoners by the militia in the spring of 1798. It is important to note that many, if not most, of the actual militiamen were Catholics. They were apparently determined to prove that, unlike their neighbors, they were loyal to the Crown. [22]

Father John Murphy, a Catholic priest, took command of the rebellion in the south. Following the French model, Murphy quickly set up a republican "government of Ireland" at Wexford. [23] It was, of course, more a dream than a real government. The only territory the republicans controlled was the little town of Wexford and its immediate surroundings.

But for a short time, the dream seemed to be becoming real. The republicans, who were known as the "Croppies," hoped that the rest of Ireland would soon rise up to join them, and they were expecting help from France at any moment. With French troops and naval support, they believed they might actually drive the English out at last. The rebels hung a proud green flag over Wexford as a symbol of Irish freedom.

But as the days went by, the dream became a nightmare. The French failed to arrive. The rebels grew increasingly desperate and undisciplined. They committed many atrocities against the Protestants in the area. In one incident alone, they slaughtered some three hundred innocent men, women, and children they had been keeping as captives since the rebellion began.

The government responded to the rebellion with equal cruelty. A triumphant Protestant song gleefully described the government's brutal response to one rebel attempt to surrender:

These rebels the country they thought to seduce—
They sent Bold MacManus with a flag of truce.
They thought that the army good terms would give,
But their answer was, "Croppies, we won't let you
live!"[24]

Rebellion also broke out in Ulster. But the men who were to lead the planned revolt there had already been betrayed and arrested. As a result, the uprising in the north was small, disorganized, and ineffective. So it is probably not true, as a bitter Catholic song complained, "Ah, Father Murphy, had aid come over / A green flag [would have] floated from shore to shore."[25]

In fact, aid *did* come over, but it was too little and too late. Once again the French sent ships to Ireland to help the rebels fight France's enemy England. This time, some French troops actually landed on Irish soil. But by then the Irish rebels were already beaten. The French ships themselves were soon defeated in a naval battle off the coast of Ireland. Wolfe Tone, who was aboard one of the French ships, was captured. He later killed himself in a British prison.[26] Other captured leaders of the rebellion were hanged.

There was one last try to achieve the United Irishmen's dream in midsummer of 1803. On July 23, a small force of fewer than one hundred rebels, led by a young ex–United Irishman named Robert Emmet, stormed historic Dublin Castle. They hoped that their brave charge would set off a general uprising throughout Ireland. It didn't. Instead, Emmet was captured a few weeks later and was eventually hanged.

Emmet is not a major figure in Irish history. His little rebellion was hopeless from the start. But he is a major figure in Irish myth. His brief, doomed gesture appeals to the romantic spirit of Irish Catholics hungry for martyrs. A true idealist, he was only in his mid-twenties when he made a powerful speech from his own gallows—a speech that has stirred pride and rebellion in Irish hearts for almost two centuries. "Let no man write my epitaph," he declared in its most famous phrase, until Ireland "takes her place among the nations of the earth. . . ."[27]

Robert Emmet's bravery and idealism helped ensure that the dream of republicanism did not die with him. But, in fact, any immediate chance to establish an Irish republic had already died years before.

THE POWER OF MYTH

William of Orange, James II, Father John Murphy of Wexford, Wolfe Tone, and Robert Emmet are creatures of myth as well as of history. As real human beings, they are long since dead. A record of their actions is tucked away in books that few people ever read. But as mythical heroes and villains, they continue to inspire—and to enrage—many people in Ulster today.

It is widely believed in Ireland that July 1, 1690, was a decisive date in Irish history. That was the day the forces of the Protestant William of Orange defeated the forces of the Catholic King James II in the Battle of the Boyne. For many of Ulster's Protestants, July 1 remains the most important holiday on the Irish calendar. Recently, some sixty thousand Orangemen flocked to the annual reenactment of the battle in the village of Scarva. Hundreds of thousands more Protestants took part in other celebrations throughout Northern Ireland, as they do every year.[28] The Orangemen and their friends use it as an annual opportunity to revel in Protestant domination over the Catholics in Ulster. Not surprisingly, this revelry is resented by many Catholics. Old hostilities are reinforced on both sides.

As a matter of historical fact, as the Irish journalist Gary MacEoin has written, "the Boyne was simply a rearguard action—and a successful one—to protect James's army while it withdrew to defensible positions." But in Northern Ireland, as MacEoin has also pointed out, "History has little bearing on myths which have acquired a life and dynamism of their own."[29]

Both the history and the myth are still alive in Northern Ireland. Many Catholics there still bitterly regret that Dermot MacMurrough ever invited Lord Strongbow across the Irish Sea. The Catholics still remember the cruelty of Oliver Cromwell, and the Protestants still remember the viciousness of Portadown. And—in a very real sense—the Battle of the Boyne, the Wexford rebellion, the uprising of the United Irishmen, and the revolt of Robert Emmet are all still being fought out today.

3

HOME RULE AND THE BIRTH
OF NORTHERN IRELAND

In some ways, Ulster has been a distinct region for centuries. It was different from the rest of Ireland in at least two ways. The first was its high proportion of Presbyterians, the descendants of the Scottish settlers who had come to Ireland in the 1600s. The second was the city of Belfast, a center of linen manufacturing and shipbuilding, whose industrial economy was very different from the agricultural economy of most of Ireland.

Most of the time, however, the divisions between Ulster and the rest of the country seemed little more than cracks in the rich Irish soil. They were real, but they were hidden by the tangle of cultural and political realities that tied the country together, including a shared resentment of England. But in the nineteenth and early twentieth centuries, a political earthquake occurred that turned those cracks into chasms. That earthquake was the coming of Irish independence.

CATHOLIC EMANCIPATION

Irish Catholics finally won back their political rights in the late 1820s, thanks largely to the efforts of a Dublin lawyer named Daniel O'Connell. O'Connell founded the Catholic Association to fight for "Catholic emancipation" in 1823. Five years later, he won election to the British Parliament from County Clare. As a Catholic, however, he was forbidden to take his seat in Westminster by the remaining Penal Laws. His election forced the issue, and in 1829 Parliament passed the Catholic Emancipation Act, granting full political rights to Catholics within the United Kingdom.

One of the most famous public speakers in Irish history, O'Connell was famous for holding "monster meetings" to rally support for home rule and for establishment of a true Irish parliament at Dublin. Huge crowds of Catholics turned out for these meetings, the largest ever seen in Ireland. They knew that now that Catholics had the right to vote, an Irish parliament would be dominated by Catholics.

The movement for Catholic Emancipation frightened the Presbyterians, who had once been the Catholics' natural allies. The Catholics outnumbered them badly. What if the Catholics' political power grew to match their numbers? What if the Catholics won power and demanded back the lands that had once belonged to them? Many of those lands—particularly the lands in Ulster—were in Presbyterian hands.

The Presbyterians were not the only ones who viewed O'Connell's movement with alarm. So did the government in London.

The British government forbade what was expected to be the largest of all the monster meetings in 1843. O'Connell called it off. Even so, he was thrown into jail for agitating against the government. The British House of Lords overturned O'Connell's conviction in 1844, and he was set free. But by then his influence had faded. [1]

Despite O'Connell's fiery speeches, he was a reformer, not a revolutionary. His failure to win home rule by peaceful means drove many Catholics into more radical, revolutionary movements. Even O'Connell's own Catholic Association turned radical.

The same process did not occur to the same extent among the Protestants. From that time on, political controversies in Ireland tended to divide more or less along Catholic-Protestant lines. And, since most of the people in Ulster were Presbyterians, while most of the people in the rest of Ireland were Catholics, Ulster found itself increasingly at odds with the rest of the country.

THE GREAT FAMINE

Ireland was an agricultural country. More than two-thirds of the Irish people were farmers, and most of them grew potatoes. In 1845, the Irish potato crop was hit by a killing blight (or disease). In 1846, the entire crop failed. A partial blight struck in 1847, and the next year the entire crop failed again.[2]

For the tenant farmers of Ireland, most of whom lived on the edge of poverty in the best of times, the failure of the potato crop was a disaster. "Language utterly fails me," wrote a Quaker relief worker trying to describe the conditions in Ireland in 1847. "My hand trembles as I write."[3] In a country of only 8,500,000 people, between 1,000,000 and 2,000,000 of them died of starvation or disease.[4] At least 1,000,000 more left the country in desperation. Ireland was devastated.

The Great Potato Famine emphasized the divisions in Irish society and made them worse. Among those divisions were growing differences between the north and the south. Although all regions suffered from the

During the Great Potato Famine, millions of Irish starved, and the country was devastated.

national disaster, the northern city of Belfast had the advantage of its linen and shipbuilding industries to fall back on. As a result, it suffered less from the famine than did most of the country.

More importantly, however, the famine increased the distrust and hatred Catholic peasants throughout the country felt toward their Protestant landlords. Even in the worst of the famine, when thousands of peasants were dying in agony every day, the landlords continued to send Irish grain to England.

That grain could have saved the lives of the starving peasants who had grown it, but the peasants had no money to pay for it. The merchants in England and elsewhere did. The Protestant landlords were businessmen. They preferred to sell their grain at a profit to saving the lives of their tenants.[5]

Bitterness against England grew along with bitterness against the landlords. The British Parliament not only failed to stop the landlords from sending food out of Ireland, it was reluctant to send any other food in. Early in the famine, a leading government official declared, "It is not the intention at all to import food for the use of the people of Ireland."[6]

The government finally gave in midway through the famine, when suffering was at its worst, and a little food was sent. But even that help was soon halted. As Charles Trevelyan, Britain's assistant secretary to the treasury, explained, "The only way to prevent people from becoming habitually dependent on government is to bring operations to a close."[7]

A few public works projects were started to provide jobs and a little money to the peasants. But, like the food aid, they were pitifully inadequate.

Why didn't England help any more than it did? For one thing, help went against the economic philosophy of the British government, which believed in laissez-faire, the idea that a government shouldn't meddle in the economic affairs of private citizens. Besides, food for Ireland was a drain on the British treasury.

But there was more to the British attitude than economics. Anti-Irish prejudice was strong among the upper-class Britons who ran the government. Many agreed with the late British economist, Thomas Malthus, that the Irish were not fully human.[8]

And, human or not, they were not to be trusted. Right to the end, there was a conviction among many British government officials that the Irish peasants were taking advantage of the situation in some way to cheat the government out of relief money. Hundreds of thousands of corpses were not enough to convince some of these officials that the suffering was real.[9]

But the suffering *was* real, and it led to immense anger and bitterness in Ireland. In 1848, a group known as Young Ireland, led by a middle-aged member of Parliament named William Smith O'Brien, attempted a revolt. Like the other Irish uprisings before it, it was more romantic than effective. Its one military attack—on some policemen in County Tipperary—failed miserably.[10]

THE BATTLE OVER HOME RULE

The calls for self-government grew louder and louder during the famine and its aftermath. In 1870, an Irish lawyer named Isaac Butt founded the Home Rule League to campaign for real self-government for Ireland. Another agricultural depression that hit Ireland in 1873 sent new recruits flooding into Butt's movement. Its growing membership led to growing political power—and not just inside Ireland. Several Irish supporters of home rule were elected to the British Parliament.

One of them was a fiery Irish nationalist named Charles Stewart Parnell. Parnell was the leader of the Land League, an organization dedicated to land reform in Ireland. The Land League promoted rent boycotts by encouraging Irish peasants to withhold the huge rents charged by their absentee landlords. The rent boycotts were often accompanied by violence.

The landlords appealed to the British government. The Land League was outlawed, and Parnell and several other leaders were thrown into Kilmainham Jail in Dublin. They were not alone. Using powers granted to them under a harsh Coercion Act, the British authorities had been cracking down on the rebellious Irish. By April 1882, there were over six hundred Irish protesters in prison.[11]

Parnell and the government worked out an agreement, known as the Kilmainham Treaty. The prisoners were released in return for a pledge that they would abandon the strategy of rent boycotts and appeal for an end to violence. In return, the government promised to move toward land reform. Any goodwill that might have come from the treaty was quickly undermined, however, by new violence committed by supporters of Irish independence.

Nonetheless, by 1885, there were eighty-six Home Rulers in the British House of Commons. Although only a minority of the total members, they found themselves holding the balance of power between the major parties.

Under the British parliamentary system, the party with the most seats in the House of Commons picks the prime minister and forms the government. If the party in power loses an important vote, a new election must be held and a new prime minister chosen. In 1885, the government was led by the Liberal Party under Prime Minister William Gladstone. Gladstone had supported land reform in Ireland, but not home rule. The eighty-six Home Rulers used their votes to help the rival Conservative Party bring down Gladstone's government. Gladstone learned his political lesson. By the time he won a new election and formed a new government in 1886, he was a supporter of home rule.

Gladstone introduced several Home Rule bills in Parliament. The first was rejected. The second was debated by the House of Commons for eighty-two days and finally passed, in the midst of a violent "disorderly melee."[12] Even so, it was rejected by the stubbornly conservative House of Lords and never became law. Unable to come up with a bill that would satisfy either the Irish Home Rulers in Parliament or the English conservatives in the House of Lords, much less both of them, Gladstone resigned in 1894.

A third Home Rule bill passed the House of Commons after one of the most bitter parliamentary battles in British history in 1912. Once again, the House of Lords rejected it. But the Liberal majority in the House of Commons, led now by Prime Minister Herbert Henry Asquith, was determined to settle the issue. They promised to bring the bill up for another vote. If the House of Commons passed the bill three times, it would become law, whether the House of Lords accepted it or not.

Protestants in the north of Ireland were outraged. The more radical of them joined an armed group called the Ulster Volunteers. They vowed to form a separate government in Ulster if Ireland were granted home rule. The bill came up again in 1914. This time, the

House of Lords agreed to accept it, but only on the condition that the six Ulster counties with Protestant majorities would remain within the United Kingdom. (The other three counties of the ancient province had Catholic majorities.)

The controversy was still raging when World War I broke out. As part of the general effort to present a united front, a limited Home Rule bill passed both houses with little or no opposition. The government, however, made two compromises with the bill's previous opponents. Home rule was not to come until after the war, and not until something was done to satisfy the angry Protestants in Ulster.

THE EASTER UPRISING

The Irish nationalists were far from satisfied by the government's plans. They didn't care about the British war effort, and they didn't trust the British to keep their promises. Besides, they wanted a lot more than limited home rule anyway. They wanted independence. Faced with a Britain distracted by war in Europe, some of the nationalists were thinking of rebellion.

Among them were the members of a small party that called itself Sinn Fein (Gaelic for "ourselves alone"); a secret society calling itself the Irish Republican Brotherhood; and two paramilitary groups, the Irish National Volunteers and the Irish Citizen Army. Members of these four groups planned an armed uprising for Easter Monday, April 24, 1916.

That morning, some two thousand rebels seized key government buildings in Dublin. A green flag with the words "Irish Republic" on it was raised over the post office. But within days, British troops arrived in

Dublin. After five days of vicious fighting in the city's streets, the Easter uprising was put down. In that short time, more than thirteen hundred people on both sides had been killed. [13]

Like all the other Irish rebellions before it, the Easter uprising was doomed from the start. For one thing, it was almost entirely confined to the Dublin area. And, even there, the rebels got little support from the general public. With hundreds of thousands of Irishmen fighting and dying under the British flag in Europe, it seemed the wrong time to take up arms against Britain.

But harsh British retaliation for the Easter uprising helped turn public sympathy in favor of the rebels. Thousands of people were arrested. Seventeen rebel leaders—including a prominent diplomat, Sir Roger Casement—were executed. One of them, who'd been so badly wounded he could not stand up for his own execution, was tied to a chair to make a suitable target for the firing squad. [14] In many Irish eyes, these men became martyrs, and the Easter uprising became one of the most powerful elements of the republican myth.

THE DAIL

Demand for independence became stronger than ever in the wake of the Easter Rising. People flocked to the banner of Sinn Fein—the only legal political party that was calling for Irish independence. In the first elections held after the war, in 1918, Sinn Fein candidates won almost three-quarters of the Irish seats in Parliament (73 of 105). [15] But instead of going to London, they set up their own parliament in Dublin, which they called the Dail Eireann, or Irish Assembly. The Dail

A view of Sackville Street in Dublin following the uprising on Easter Monday, April 24, 1916

*The Sinn Fein flag prominently displayed
in Dublin in 1917. Sinn Fein was the original
Irish Nationalist Party, traditionally
associated with the IRA.*

promptly declared independence. On April 1, 1919, it elected Eamon de Valera, who'd been a leader of the Easter Rising, as the first head of the new "government" of the Republic of Ireland.

THE VIEW FROM
THE NORTH

There was support for the independence movement— and opposition to it—throughout the country. A strong majority of Catholics everywhere had voted for Sinn Fein. Many who did not belong to the IRA (Irish Republican Army) themselves did things to help it, some of them directly, some indirectly. There was even sympathy for independence among some Protestants. At the same time, there were Catholics who opposed independence, and even more who were disgusted by the violent methods of the IRA. But, in general, most Catholics favored independence, and most Protestants opposed it.

In the north, as elsewhere, opinions tended to follow old religious and cultural lines. But in Ulster, the proportions were reversed. A strong majority, particularly among the Anglo-Protestants, bitterly opposed independence. What would happen to them—a resented minority in the country they had lived in for centuries—without the strong arm of Britain to protect them?

INCREASING VIOLENCE

It was a complicated situation. As far as the English and the Protestants in the north were concerned, all of Ireland was still a part of the United Kingdom, ruled from London. And yet the Dail continued to meet, declaring itself the ruling body of a free Ireland. Michael Collins, the minister of finance appointed by the Dail, even arranged large foreign loans for the new government.

All sides knew that this standoff could not go on forever. Among the nationalists, the Irish National Volunteers, led by Michael Collins, were determined to force the issue. Calling themselves the Irish Republican Army, they began launching guerrilla attacks on members of the ten-thousand-man Royal Irish Constabulary, or RIC—the national police force. Roving "flying squads" of IRA killers traveled the countryside on bicycles searching out their victims. Over the next few years, scores of policemen and other officials were shot down by the IRA, many of them from ambush.

The police sometimes fought back with similar tactics. On one occasion, the republican mayor of the town of Cork was assassinated in cold blood by a gang of RIC constables wearing masks. [16]

Meanwhile, in the north, militant Protestants (many of them from the lodges of the secret Orange Order) carried out attacks of their own against IRA sympathizers.

A private Protestant army called the Ulster Volunteers had already been founded by Edward Carson in 1912. They had fought bravely alongside British troops in Europe in World War I. Home in Ulster, they threatened to fight to the death against any British effort to grant home rule. They held public military drills to intimidate the Catholics and the British government alike. They loudly announced that Ulster would never be part of an "independent" Ireland. If London granted Irish independence, they declared, Ulster would secede. There would be civil war.

THE GOVERNMENT OF
IRELAND ACT

The British Parliament tried to satisfy all sides by the Government of Ireland Act of 1920. This act established two separate Irish parliaments. One was to be in Dublin, the other in Belfast. In this way, both the largely Catholic south and the mostly Protestant north would each have a degree of self-government. But both Irish parliaments would remain under the overall authority of the Parliament in London, keeping ultimate control of all of Ireland in British hands. [17]

The Dublin parliament called for in the Government of Ireland Act of 1920 never actually met. There was too much opposition to it in the Catholic south. But England's King George V traveled to Belfast to open the north's new parliament on June 22, 1921. It was, of course, completely dominated by Protestant loyalists who were determined to keep Ulster within the United Kingdom.

If the government was hoping its two-parliament scheme would bring peace to Ireland, it was soon disappointed. The nationalists wanted nothing less than a truly independent Irish republic, while the loyalists in the north feared that the scheme was just the first step in a British plan to desert them altogether. All sides increased their violent activities. IRA violence became so great, in fact, that this period in Irish history is sometimes known as the Anglo-Irish War.

THE BLACK AND TANS

The job of fighting the IRA fell to the forty thousand or so British troops in Ireland[18] and to Ireland's own police forces: the Metropolitan Police, who were responsible for law and order in Dublin, and the RIC, who were responsible for keeping the peace everywhere else.

Even together, these groups were not equal to the task. The British army was trained to fight other armies, not individual terrorists and small groups of men on bicycles. And the Irish police were less than reliable. Many of them were sympathetic to the republican cause themselves, and even many of those who weren't were reluctant to battle their nationalist neighbors and friends.

The British government decided to reinforce the RIC with "temporary" constables recruited in England. Their uniforms were khaki brown, with black boots and belts, so the Irish dubbed them the "Black and Tans." Being neither regular Army nor police, these newcomers were almost as outside the law as the IRA guerrillas they fought. They were not subject to the Irish courts, nor even to the rules and regulations of the British army. Lacking such restraints, they earned a reputation for cruelty and lack of discipline. In a country already torn by hatred between religious, political, and military groups, the Black and Tans became the most hated group of all.

Even the RIC didn't want them. A number of its highest-ranking officials resigned rather than work with them. For many Irish citizens, the kidnappings and murders committed by the IRA and the Protestant terrorists taken together were overshadowed by the outrages committed by the Black and Tans. On November 21, 1920, for example, a band of them fired into a crowd at a soccer match and killed fourteen people.[19]

British troops in Dublin in 1920

But no matter how vicious they were, the Black and Tans could not win the Anglo-Irish War any more than the British army and the Irish police could.

THE ANGLO-IRISH TREATY

In 1921, the British prime minister, Lloyd George, suggested a peace conference.[20] An Irish delegation headed by Michael Collins, the mastermind of the IRA terrorism, met with British government officials in London. The result was the Anglo-Irish Treaty, signed on December 6, 1921.

This treaty established a new country in the south called the Irish Free State. Although the new nation would remain within the British Commonwealth, it would be governed by its own, all-Irish parliament at Dublin. Technically, it would have the same essentially independent status within the Commonwealth that Canada and Australia enjoyed. In 1949, it would join the Commonwealth and officially become known as the Republic of Ireland. Ireland was independent at last.

But England had not deserted her friends in the north. The Irish Free State would include only twenty-six of Ireland's counties. The others—the six heavily Protestant counties of Armagh, Down, Antrim, (London)Derry, Tyrone, and Fermanagh—would have the option of remaining under the authority and protection of Great Britain. It was an option that the Belfast parliament rushed to take, quickly reaffirming the existence of Northern Ireland, as it had first been established by the Government of Ireland Act in 1920.[21]

THE IRISH CIVIL WAR

For the next two years, civil war raged in both Irelands. Although the Anglo-Irish Treaty was passed by the Dail and confirmed by the first election in the Irish Free State, many nationalists still bitterly opposed the treaty. They did not want Ireland to be in the British Commonwealth at all. What is more, they rejected Ulster's right to opt out of the Irish Free State. They were determined to reunite Ireland under one flag.

The government of the Irish Free State was committed to the Anglo-Irish Treaty. After all, it only came into existence as a result of it. Even so, many of the nationalist politicians—including Eamon de Valera himself—refused to accept it.

The IRA, which had fought long and hard for an independent Ireland, split on the issue. One large faction, led by Michael Collins, supported the treaty. Another opposed it.

During those bloody first years of Northern Ireland's existence, 232 people were killed and 1,000 more were wounded in the fighting over the treaty.[22] Catholics, who made up only one-third of the population, made up two-thirds of the victims of this violence.[23]

In 1925, an agreement was signed between Northern Ireland, the United Kingdom, and the Irish Free State. It reaffirmed the existence of Northern Ireland and officially established its legal borders.

More importantly, the great majority of both Catholics and Protestants seemed to accept the existence of two Irelands—even if they didn't like it. Certainly most Protestants in the north were relieved not to be a part of what they saw as the Catholic Free State. And in the south, Catholic voters in the elections of 1927 indicated that they, too, accepted the government established by the Anglo-Irish Treaty.

The issue seemed settled. At least for a while.

4

IN SEARCH OF
A GOVERNMENT—FROM
STORMONT TO LONDON

The parliament established for Northern Ireland under the Government of Ireland Act was known as Stormont. It was named for the Belfast suburb in which the government buildings were located. Stormont governed Ulster for more than fifty years, until the British ordered it disbanded in the early 1970s. Throughout its history, it was controlled by the Unionist Party.

The Unionists had been the majority political party in Ulster since the days of the home rule fight. Then, as now, the party spoke for the loyalists—the majority of Protestants who want to keep Ulster inside the United Kingdom, and to keep themselves from being swallowed up by the south's Catholic majority.

Then, as now, the Unionists kept their power by hammering at the wedge of fear and suspicion that has long existed between the Protestants and Catholics in Ulster. As the Irish authors and historians Maire and Conor Cruise O'Brien have written:

"Politically, Protestant fears of a Catholic threat became the stock-in-trade of the Unionist Party. These fears have furnished that party with an unbroken mo-

*In ceremonies in 1949 marking the final break
with British rule after eight centuries,
the president of the Republic of Ireland
reviews honor guard in a public square.
The end of British rule was cause for great
celebration among the Irish.*

nopoly of political power, through the support of almost the whole Protestant population, since the foundation of Northern Ireland."[1]

When Stormont finally fell, it was not because of any change in the Unionist majority in Northern Ireland. The Unionists are still the most powerful political party in Ulster. It fell because it could not, or would not, control the Troubles—the waves of violence and hatred that broke over Ulster in the 1960s, and that are still crashing over it today.

THE CIVIL RIGHTS MOVEMENT

Ironically, the Troubles that have brought so much violence and death to Northern Ireland were touched off by a peaceful, nonviolent movement for civil rights.

Northern Ireland has always been the poorest partner in the United Kingdom. Economic problems—unemployment, poor housing, inadequate health care—have always been worse for the people of Ulster than for the residents of England, Scotland, or Wales. And, within Ulster, they have always been worse for most Catholics than for most Protestants.

This is hardly surprising in a province with such a long and bitter history of hostility between Catholics and Protestants—and one in which Protestants have held almost all the political and economic power.

According to the O'Briens, the use of Protestant power "was unspectacular but effective. Key localities with Catholic majorities were gerrymandered to produce Protestant councils: these councils in turn gave jobs and houses to Protestants in preference to Catholics."[2]

It was this discrimination, more than anything else, that led to the start of the current Troubles in the

1960s. In January 1967, a number of Catholics, along with some sympathetic Protestants, banded together to found NICRA, the Northern Ireland Civil Rights Association.3 Inspired by the example of the U.S. civil rights movement, they decided to try some of its nonviolent tactics in Northern Ireland. They hoped that peaceful marches and other public demonstrations would bring improvements in employment, housing, and voting rights for Catholics. In addition, they demanded an end to the B-Specials, the semiamateur police squads the Catholics claimed were running roughshod over their neighborhoods.

Somewhere between 2,500 and 4,000 people took part in NICRA's first civil rights march, ending in Dungannon, in August 1968. In a sign of confrontation to come, some 1,500 loyalists held a meeting of their own nearby.4

The police kept the two groups away from each other in Dungannon, but the potential for violence was obvious. When NICRA scheduled another march for (London)Derry in October, the government banned it. When the marchers went ahead anyway, police waded into them with batons, setting off riots that went on all night.

The government, under Prime Minister Terence O'Neill, introduced a plan for reforms. O'Neill himself went on television with a historic plea to the people of Northern Ireland.

"Ulster stands at the crossroads," he declared. "In Londonderry and other places recently, a minority of agitators determined to subvert lawful authority played a part in setting light to highly inflammable material. But the tinder for that fire, in the form of grievances real or imaginary, had been piling up for years.

"What kind of Ulster do you want?" he asked. "A

happy and respected Province, in good standing with the rest of the United Kingdom? Or a place continually torn apart by riots and demonstrations, and regarded by the rest of Britain as a political outcast? As always in a democracy, the choice is yours."[5]

But the choice would not be made democratically by all the people, but by a minority of angry extremists. Many of them were within O'Neill's own Unionist Party. Although 150,000 messages of support poured into O'Neill's office,[6] he was soon forced to resign as prime minister by his Unionist colleagues in Stormont.[7]

THE BATTLE LINES
ARE DRAWN

The new prime minister the Unionists picked to replace O'Neill was James D. Chichester-Clark. He was considered a hard-liner, someone not likely to compromise. But he was more moderate than Brian Faulkner, whom he had defeated for the office by one vote.[8] It wouldn't be long, however, before Chichester-Clark, too, was forced from office and Faulkner took his place. The battle lines between the loyalist Protestants and the nationalist Catholics were being drawn more clearly all the time.

Both the Catholics and Protestants were taking to the streets. Clashes began to occur. In some of them, the police of the Royal Ulster Constabulary seemed to side with the loyalists. (The Royal Ulster Constabulary, or RUC, was the successor to the Royal Irish Constabulary of earlier days.) In January 1967, a civil rights march by university students was attacked by Protestants with sticks and clubs. The Protestants were led by a radical Orangeman, the Reverend Ian Paisley. Originally a Presbyterian minister, Paisley had decided his church was not nearly anti-Catholic enough. Resigning, he'd started his own sect, which he called the Free Presbyterian Church of Ulster. He had already been in jail once for promoting anti-Catholic rioting in 1964, and he would soon go to jail again.

The Catholics had found an unlikely but powerful leader of their own in a woman named Bernadette Devlin. A member of the Young Socialist Alliance, Devlin was only twenty years old when she won a seat in the British House of Commons in 1969. Nonetheless, she electrified Britain with her first speech in Parliament, in which she explained the situation in Northern Ireland from an angry Catholic point of view. "There is no place for us, the ordinary peasant, in Northern Ireland," she declared. "It is a society of the landlords."[9]

Like Paisley, Devlin would soon be jailed for promoting riots. And, like Devlin, Paisley would soon be elected to the British House of Commons.

The Northern Ireland government at Stormont and the British government in London issued a joint declaration in August 1969. In it, they insisted that "every citizen of Northern Ireland is entitled to the same equality of treatment and freedom from discrimination as obtains in the rest of the United Kingdom irrespective of political views or religion."[10] But the Catholics were unconvinced. The worst riots of all took place in (London)Derry and Belfast that same month.

London sent army troops to both cities to help keep the peace.[11] But almost as soon as the riots broke out in Belfast, the authorities on the scene called out the B-Specials. They proceeded to roam through the Falls Road neighborhoods, shooting off guns and setting fire to houses. Eight people, including two children, were

Right: British soldiers check residents' belongings at a roadblock in Belfast in 1969. The barbed wire was to keep Protestants and Catholics apart in the Falls Road area, the scene of some of the worst rioting. Below: In the twenty years since the late 1960s, there has been an intensification of the violence on all sides of the Irish conflict and an increase in polarization among the population.

killed. [12] Altogether, hundreds were injured in three days of street fighting before British troops managed to restore order.

THE BRITISH ARMY TO THE RESCUE?

The British troops were warmly welcomed by the Catholics, who saw them as protectors. After all, most of the riots had been caused by attacks on peace marchers. And, for a time, the British troops also seemed to see their role as protecting the Catholics from Protestant extremists.

But the IRA was becoming increasingly active. And the IRA did not see the British troops as protectors. As more troops continued to arrive, the IRA worked to convince the Catholics that the troops were an invading army occupying Ulster.

In January 1970, the IRA split in two. One branch, calling itself the Official IRA, announced that it would not participate in terrorism. Although it supported the "armed struggle," it said it would work for the same goals with the more peaceful methods of argument and political organization. The Provisional branch of the IRA, on the other hand, went underground. The Provos vowed to continue, and even to increase, their attacks on the security forces.

Meanwhile, a new loyalist group called the Ulster Defence Association (or UDA) began carrying out similar attacks on the other side.

Many Unionists saw no difference between the civil rights demonstrators, the rioters, and the terrorists of the IRA. Some, in fact, thought that the civil rights demonstrations had never been anything but a respectable front for the terrorists.

A commission set up by the British government to study the riots decided the Unionists were wrong. It reported that yes, the IRA supported the demonstrators and took part in the demonstrations. But the IRA was only a part of the movement, it did not control it. [13] It wasn't long, however, before the outrages of the Provos and the Ulster Defence Association came to overshadow any peaceful efforts on either side.

As IRA violence increased, British troops were more often called into action against the IRA. Many Catholics—those who supported the aims of the IRA, if not its methods—began viewing the British with more caution, and even hostility. Suspicion of the British became even greater in 1970, when the Conservative Party took over the government of Great Britain. The Catholics were aware that the British Conservatives had always had close ties with Ulster's Unionist Party.

Suddenly, in 1971, the government started throwing suspected troublemakers in jail. The reason for the new policy was not entirely clear. It was, perhaps, partly the result of the stepped-up violence of the IRA and partly the result of the new British government's sympathy with the Protestants.

Whatever the reason, the nationalists were outraged. Internment (jailing without trial) was clearly directed against them. Of the more than three hundred people who were arrested in the first sweep on August 9, only two were Protestants. [14] Since the British army had the job of carrying out the policy, it soon lost most of the gratitude it had won earlier from the Catholics.

Whatever little good feeling was left was wiped out by the tragic events of "Bloody Sunday"—January 30, 1972. On that day, thousands of nationalists defied a government ban on all demonstrations in Catholic

Faces masked to prevent identification, a squad of the outlawed IRA patrols an area in (London)-Derry. The IRA's aim is to unite the six counties of British-ruled Northern Ireland with the predominantly Roman Catholic Irish Republic.

(London)Derry and staged a march to protest internment.

Before the march was over, British troops fired into the crowd. Exactly what started the shooting isn't clear. Some of the nationalists were throwing stones. The troops were using tear gas. The army later claimed that it had been fired on first. Nationalist observers denied that this happened. In any case, the troops opened fire on the crowd, and thirteen of the demonstrators were shot dead in the street. Later investigations indicated that most—if not all—of the dead had been unarmed. [15]

The shootings in (London)Derry caused intense outrage among Catholics on both sides of the Irish border. Three days later, the Republic of Ireland declared a day of mourning for the thirteen people who had been killed. Breaking off from a peaceful march in memory of the victims, a mob attacked the British embassy in Dublin and set it on fire. [16]

The IRA stepped up its terrorist activities in February 1972. A Protestant member of Stormont was wounded in an assassination attempt, while two Irishmen serving in the British army and two members of a loyalist terrorist group were murdered. The IRA terror even reached into England. On February 22, a car bomb killed seven people near the officers' mess (dining hall) of a British parachute regiment in Aldershot. Ironically, the only British officer among them was a Roman Catholic chaplain. [17]

DIRECT RULE

The British government decided that things were getting entirely out of hand in Northern Ireland. From Britain's point of view, the Stormont parliament was unable to control the situation in Ulster. Something had to be done.

In March 1972, the British Parliament passed the Northern Ireland (Temporary Provisions) Act. It suspended the Stormont parliament and gave the government of the United Kingdom—that is, the Parliament at Westminster—the power to govern Northern Ireland directly. Responsibility for the job was put in the hands of a newly established secretary of state for Northern Ireland.[18] The next year, Britain abolished the Stormont parliament altogether. Northern Ireland has been under direct rule from London ever since.

Reaction to direct rule was mixed in both communities. Northern Ireland was being treated like a child, unable to look after itself. On the other hand, most people could see that, in reality, Ulster had not looked after itself very well.

Most people, Protestants and Catholics alike, seemed willing to accept at least temporary direct rule, even if they were not happy with it. It was not a final solution to the Troubles, but it might be better than what had gone before. It might provide a chance for tempers to cool down and for the various sides in the struggle to work out a long-term solution to the problem themselves.

But, while most residents of Ulster accepted direct rule, the extremists on both sides rejected it totally. The loyalist hard-liners who controlled Stormont did not want their seat of power taken away from them, even by the British. Two hundred thousand Protestant workers staged a two-day strike to show their opposition.[19] The IRA, meanwhile, would not accept British rule of any kind. As we will see in the next chapter, direct rule failed to bring an end to the terrorism by either side. It may even have encouraged it.

In June 1989, more than seventeen years after it was first imposed, the British Parliament renewed the direct rule legislation for the fifteenth time. The current secretary of state for Northern Ireland, Tom King, admitted that direct rule was neither democratic nor satisfactory. "[I]t is on all our consciences," he said, "that we have still not found a better alternative."[20]

SEARCHING FOR AN ALTERNATIVE

Ever since Stormont was abolished, attempts have been made to set up some new system of government to replace it. The first efforts established a seventy-eight-member, elected Northern Ireland Assembly in 1973. It was, of course, dominated by the loyalist Unionist Party. A smaller executive council was added to the system in 1974. Intended to reflect a wider range of opinion in Ulster, it included several nationalist, as well as loyalist, members.

As a solid majority, the Unionists were angered by this effort to make them share political power in Ulster. They torpedoed the executive council at every turn. Following a strike by loyalists throughout Ulster, the executive council was disbanded in May 1974.

A constitutional convention was elected in 1975 to "consider what provision for the government of Northern Ireland is likely to command the most widespread acceptance among the community."[21] It apparently concluded that no form of government was "likely to command widespread acceptance" in Ulster, because it ended in dismal failure in 1976.

A new assembly was elected in 1982, under a scheme that ensured the election of at least some nationalist members. It had little real power, but there was hope it might come up with a plan that would lead to a more practical form of government for Ulster in the future. But this assembly, too, was doomed from the start.

The loyalists controlled the new assembly, just as they had the old one. Despairing of having an effective role in the assembly, the nonloyalist members boycotted its meetings. Finally, angered by an agreement between Britain and the Republic of Ireland in 1986, even the loyalists refused to carry out their duties as members. Recognizing still another failure, Britain eventually abolished the assembly altogether.[22]

THE ANGLO-IRISH AGREEMENT

Neither the nationalists nor the unionists agree about everything, even among themselves. There are some in each group who are moderate, some who are radical (extreme). Some are dedicated socialists, some capitalists, and some have no interest in economic matters beyond their own jobs and the price of food.

But what each group wants most has always been clear. The nationalists want the English to leave, and Ulster to be reunited with the rest of Ireland. The Unionists want Ulster to stay a part of the United Kingdom.

But what do England and the Republic of Ireland want?

Officially, the British government claims that it has no selfish interest in Ulster. It spends more on social services there than it could ever get back, and it pays a high price in lives and property lost to the terrorists by staying there. Its only reason for all this, says Westminster, is to honor its commitment to the Protestant majority in Ulster. And it insists that it will stay there as long as that majority wants it to remain.

But neither the Unionists nor the nationalists fully believe what London says. Many nationalists believe that England really wants to keep Northern Ireland as its last colony, the way a master might want to keep a slave, even after the slave has outlived its usefulness. Many Ulster Protestants, on the other hand, fear that England really wants to find a way to leave and to get rid of all the problems the province represents. They know that polls show that many Britons would agree with the old Beatles song that called on Britain to "give Ireland back to the Irish." One 1988 poll, conducted for the *Economist* newspaper in Britain, found that 50 percent of Britons wanted the troops removed immediately.

The Republic of Ireland, on the other hand, has always demanded reunification with the six counties it lost in 1920. As recently as twenty years ago, the possibility of invading the north was apparently discussed in a meeting of the Republic's cabinet in Dublin.[23] But many people on both sides of the border have as little faith in Dublin's claims as they do in Westminster's.[24] They doubt the Republic's true desire for reunion—at least for reunion now.

One of the doubters is Sister Anna, an Episcopalian nun working for peace in Ulster. The "last thing" the Republic's leaders want, she says, "is to have Northern Ireland land on their plate. They've got a lot of unemployment, they've got a very ticklish economic situation, they're struggling very manfully to pull their little country into the right way. Now suddenly to be landed with all the unemployment in Northern Ireland . . . [and] a million rampant Protestants, some of whom are paramilitary—they couldn't cope."[25]

The two governments attempted to clarify their

positions in the Anglo-Irish Agreement of 1985, the same agreement that so outraged the Unionists they scuttled the assembly.

The historic document was signed by Margaret Thatcher, the prime minister of Great Britain, and Garrett Fitzgerald, the prime minister of the Irish Republic, on November 15, 1985. It was quickly passed by both parliaments and came into effect on November 29.

In it, each government made a major concession to the other. For the first time, Britain formally acknowledged that the Republic has a valid interest in the affairs of Northern Ireland and has a right to participate in its affairs. An intergovernmental conference was established, in which officials of both governments meet regularly to work out policies for Northern Ireland. Somewhere near the top of the list is increased cooperation in the battle against terrorism. Other subjects discussed include a wide range of legal, social, and economic policies—including protections for human rights; ways of improving the unhappy relations between Catholics and Protestants, as well as between Catholics and the police and military forces; the need to reduce discrimination in employment; and the possibility of increasing the use of the Irish (or Gaelic) language in the north.

For its part, the Republic agreed to Britain's insistence that there can never be reunion between the two Irelands without the consent of the majority of the people of Ulster. In effect, that means the consent of the Protestants. As a British government publication describes the understanding: "Both Governments recognised that such consent does not at present exist but that should a majority in Northern Ireland, at some future time, formally consent to the establishment of a united Ireland, they would introduce and support the necessary legislation."[26]

Both governments acknowledged that direct rule could not go on forever. Instead, they agreed to work toward a "devolved government" for Ulster. Neither government will explain what a "devolved" government will look like. (The term "devolved" means "handed on" or "turned over.") But they insist that the new government will have to be acceptable to both the nationalists and the unionists. Meanwhile, each recognizes the other's right to have a say in the "devolution" process.

REACTION TO THE ANGLO-IRISH AGREEMENT

Like every other political action in Northern Ireland, the Anglo-Irish Agreement became a center of controversy. Most people considered it a step forward for the nationalists. It gave Ulster a new political tie to the Republic, and it left the door to a future union with the Republic wide open. Because of this, most Catholics in Northern Ireland welcomed the agreement. But not all.

Sinn Fein, now a legal political party that acts as an arm of the IRA, was fiercely opposed to the agreement from the start. It considered the measures that were supposedly intended to help the Catholic population as a smokescreen to disguise the real purpose of the agreement—increased cooperation between the two governments to destroy the IRA.

But the most bitter opposition to the agreement came from the Protestants. They saw it as a betrayal— the first step in a British plan to sell them out. After

Protests to the Anglo-Irish Agreement were strongest among the Protestants. The agreement called for the Irish Republic to play a consultative role in Northern Ireland. Protestants viewed this as a first step toward Northern Ireland's absorption into a united Catholic Ireland.

helping to destroy the assembly with their boycott, the Unionists stubbornly refused to join in the "devolution" of a new government for Ulster. Four years later, in 1989, James Molyneaux, the leader of the powerful Ulster Unionist Party, is still insisting, "We will not negotiate with the Agreement in place."[27]

Predictably, the political storm over the agreement was reflected in an upsurge of violence and terrorism. Some Unionist terrorists responded to the agreement with a dramatic increase in killings and intimidation of Catholics. The Unionist terrorism prompted an equal, or greater, upsurge in nationalist terrorism. And this, in turn, has prompted harsher and harsher measures on the part of the British government to bring order to Northern Ireland. Those measures have not succeeded. The new chain of violence that began tightening around Ulster in the mid-1980s still holds that troubled land in its deadly grip today.

Neither the political uproar nor the increased violence has succeeded in destroying the agreement. After a formal review of the agreement in 1989, the British secretary of state for Northern Ireland announced, "The outcome of the review makes clear the value that both governments attach to the work of the [intergovernmental conference], and the benefit they see in that work being continued and . . . enhanced."[28] The agreement remained—and still remains—in effect. Meanwhile, the search for a government goes on.

5

NORTHERN IRELAND
TODAY

Eight centuries of bloody conflict have not spoiled the beauty of Northern Ireland. A visitor could travel around most of the country outside of Belfast without seeing any physical signs of the violence that torments it.

The countryside has a ripe, green look, the result of the lucky combination of a richly fertile soil and a damp but gentle climate. This soil and climate make possible the agriculture on which a large part of Ulster's economy is based. The great central plain that makes up most of the province's interior is a crazy quilt of small farms that grow potatoes, grains, and turnips, and small orchards that grow apples and pears. This interior region is bounded on the north and southeast by ridges of small but rugged mountains.

Ulster's 330 miles of picturesque coastline are studded with quiet coves and rocky outcroppings. The most dramatic of the coastal features is the so-called Giant's Causeway, a massive collection of nearly 40,000 flat-sided pillars of ancient volcanic basalt in County Antrim. Some of these mysterious black pillars stand as much as 20 feet high. According to local legend, they were the stepping-stones of a legendary giant named Finn McCool.[1] To the modern eye, however, they look more like a large model of a dark, futuristic city built entirely of windowless skyscrapers.

Water is everywhere in Northern Ireland. The Irish Sea beats against the coast. Brooks and streams flow down from the mountains, and even the flat inland regions are filled with marshlands and peat bogs. The many loughs (or lakes) include Lough Neagh, the largest lake in the British Isles. Among the major rivers are the Foyle, the Upper and Lower Banns, the Main, the Blackwater, and the River Lagan, which flows through Belfast.

THE TOWNS

Most of the towns in Northern Ireland are little more than villages. Their ancient high streets (or main streets) are rimmed with buildings made of stone and wood, some of which were built before Columbus sailed.

The 1980 census showed that there are only three towns in the entire province with more than fifty thousand residents. And one of them, Newtownabbey, is really a suburb of the largest, Belfast.

Mere size, however, is not the only measure of a town's importance. The town of Enniskillen, for example, is an important regional center in the western part of the country. And Armagh, in the south-central region, not far from the border with the Republic, has a special significance as a religious capital. Saint Patrick founded a church there some fifteen hundred years ago, and it has been a center of church life in Ulster ever since.

Today, there are not just one but *two* cathedrals dedicated to Saint Patrick in Armagh. One is presided over by the archbishop of the Church of Ireland and is considered the heart of the Protestant church in Northern Ireland. The other, presided over by the Roman Catholic archbishop of Ireland, is the seat of the Catholic church for all of Ireland, Northern Ireland and the Republic alike. Not surprisingly, then, the Armagh region is a major hotbed of political terrorist activity.

The second largest city in Northern Ireland is located in the northwestern corner of the country. Named Londonderry by the loyalists, it is called Derry by the nationalists. [In order to avoid taking sides in this war of words, this book has referred to it as (London)Derry.] Its major industries are shirtmaking and shipbuilding, but it is best known for being the only large town in Ulster with a Catholic—and nationalist—majority.

By far the greatest center of both population and industry is on the other side of the country, along the Irish Sea. It is there that the industrial towns of Lisburn, Portadown, and Lurgan huddle in the shadow of Northern Ireland's largest city.

BELFAST—THE DIVIDED HEART OF NORTHERN IRELAND

Over half of all the people in Northern Ireland live in or around the city of Belfast.[2] In its division of Protestants and Catholics, the population of Belfast reflects the population of Ulster as a whole. And it is there that the turmoil of the country's past and present is most clearly visible.

Like many large cities in America, Belfast is a city of neighborhoods. Some of those neighborhoods are virtual ghettos—places in which people of certain characteristics huddle together, partly from choice and partly from necessity. In America, ghetto neighborhoods are usually segregated according to race or ethnic background. In Belfast, the deciding factor is religion.

The peasants who left their farms and moved to Belfast to find work during the Great Famine arrived first on the western edge of the city. They felt out of place in their new surroundings. They were farmers, not used to the ways of a big city. And they were Catholics, newly arrived in an overwhelmingly Presbyterian Protestant town.

To make things even more uncomfortable for them, they were met with hostility from the people in the established poor neighborhoods. The workers of Belfast feared and resented the new arrivals—and with good reason. From their point of view, the newcomers were bringing poverty and unemployment north with them. They had come to compete for jobs in the city's factories, and those jobs had been scarce enough when there were only Protestant workers to compete for them.[3]

Not surprisingly, the newcomers clustered together, partly for the comfort of familiarity and partly for protection. Many settled along the Falls Road on the western outskirts of Belfast, making it a Catholic outpost on the edge of the Presbyterian city.

As it happened, the Falls Road neighborhood was right next door to a working-class Protestant neighborhood that had grown up along the nearby Shankill Road. Hostility between the two neighborhoods sprang up at once.

It is now almost a century and a half later. But those same two neighborhoods—the Catholic Falls Road and the Protestant Shankill—are still hotbeds of bitterness, hatred, and violence between Catholics and Protestants. Many terrorists on both sides were born and raised in those neighborhoods, and much of the worst violence is committed there.

Other nationalist neighborhoods include the Markets, Short Strand, Ardoyne, and Andersonstown, where the gun-and-grenade attack on the IRA funeral occurred in 1988. Loyalist neighborhoods include Sandy Row, Ballymacaret, and East Belfast.

Signs of the Troubles are most pronounced in the nationalist, Catholic neighborhoods. They are heavily patrolled by the security forces, which see them as the most likely source of further trouble.

Some neighborhoods are physically separated from the rest of the city by a crazy quilt pattern of fences, walls, and other barriers known as the peace lines. These were built by the security forces to help control possible riots. They make it possible to close off whole areas of the city and to check the identity of anyone moving in and out. The divided areas include those neighborhoods the police consider potential hotbeds of violence, as well as the downtown area of the city, which they are determined to protect.

There are three main security forces in Northern Ireland today. The Royal Ulster Constabulary (or RUC) is Ulster's regular police force. The so-called Ulster Defence Association is the successor of the hated B-Specials. And the third and largest security force is the British army. In recent years, there have probably been as many as twenty thousand British troops stationed in Northern Ireland. Today, there are around sixteen thousand.[4]

When things are tense, the security forces patrol the Catholic areas in armored trucks and tanklike per-

sonnel carriers or else march through the neighborhoods brandishing NATO self-loading rifles in a show of
force. At times like these, the forces look very much
like the invading army many nationalists believe them
to be.

Not all the neighborhoods of Belfast are either religious ghettos or potential trouble spots, however. In
the wealthier suburbs around the city, the relatively
few rich Catholics live peacefully side by side with the
more numerous wealthy Protestants. There are also
several new, middle-class suburbs springing up, in
which Protestants and Catholics live together.

ECONOMIC CONDITIONS

Work is scarce. In Belfast as a whole, one out of five
workers is jobless. In the Catholic ghettos, it is two out
of five.[5] Although there has been a slight improvement
lately, overall unemployment is still twice what it was
in 1972.

Some of the job loss in Ulster is probably due to the
atmosphere created by the Troubles. But much of it,
says Caroline Cracraft, a British consular officer with a
special concern for Ulster, would have happened anyway.[6] Traditionally, many jobs have depended on the
shipbuilding and linen industries, and both have problems that have nothing to do with Ulster's politics.

*A young boy looks at damage done to a swim
center in Belfast by an IRA bomb. For the
thousands of young people living in Northern
Ireland's most terror-ridden neighborhoods,
violence is a normal way of life.*

Much of the world's shipbuilding business has gone to Asia, while synthetic fabrics have been reducing the market for real linens.

About 42 percent of those who do work in Northern Ireland work either directly or indirectly for some level of government.[7] The British government has been working hard to attract new industry to Northern Ireland. It provides financial help to companies that invest there, ranging from reduced taxes to grants of money to help pay for building and research costs. In 1987–88, the government's Northern Ireland Industrial Development Board claims to have attracted 302 million pounds of investment to Ulster, resulting in 5,300 jobs.

Among the modern manufacturing industries represented in Northern Ireland are electronics, communications equipment, oil-well equipment, food processing and packaging, carpets, and synthetic rubber. Major American companies with branches there include Ford and General Motors, Du Pont, and Hughes Tool. Some international companies based in Europe and Japan also have plants in Ulster, providing a total of about ten thousand jobs. The single biggest employer in Ulster is an aerospace engineering firm named Short Brothers PLC, which employs about seventy-five hundred people. About nine thousand more work in the province's tourism industry.[8]

Largely because of the high unemployment rate, young people have been leaving the province. In 1986–87, the last year for which figures are available, almost six thousand people moved out. That was a rise of over 60 percent from the year before. The majority of them were between fifteen and forty-four years old.[9]

The high unemployment rate also helps explain the relatively high rate of burglaries and other forms of robbery in Belfast. Desperate people who can't find

A typical street scene in one of the poorest areas of Belfast. In some families, no one has been able to work for several generations.

work sometimes turn to theft to feed themselves and their families.

But aside from robberies, the rate of serious crime—particularly violent crime—is low. There are few murders and violent assaults, except, of course, for those committed by the terrorists. Even including terrorist crimes, though, the overall crime rate in Northern Ireland is still lower than that of the United States. [10]

SOCIAL SERVICES

Northern Ireland is a welfare state; that is, the government takes the responsibility for providing a minimum standard of food, shelter, education, and health care for all citizens.

As citizens of the United Kingdom, the people of Ulster have a right to the same government services as the people of England, Scotland, and Wales. But because of Northern Ireland's poor economy, the province cannot provide all of these things itself. As a result, much of the money for these services has come from London. In 1987–88, for example, the British government provided nearly $2 billion worth of funds for services in Ulster. Altogether, public expenditures of all kinds in 1988–89 amounted to about $5,000 for each of Northern Ireland's 1,567,000 people— considerably more per person than in the rest of the United Kingdom. [11] Despite this aid, the average life span in Northern Ireland is two years shorter than in the rest of the United Kingdom.

Despite all the money spent, the social services received by many residents of Northern Ireland are poor. The health system, for example, has been stretched far beyond its limits. News reports from Bel-

In a main shopping area of Dublin, homeless children huddle together.

fast often tell of patients being turned away from hospitals. Some have had to wait as long as eleven hours to get emergency treatment in Belfast's City Hospital. [12]

Child care is also inadequate. A study by the Equal Opportunities Commission found Northern Ireland's day-care facilities the worst in Europe. It also rated Ulster poorly in its provisions for maternity and parental leave for working parents. [13]

LIVING CONDITIONS

For the poor and the unemployed, living conditions in Northern Ireland are the worst to be found anywhere in the United Kingdom, according to the most recent housing condition survey. This is particularly true in the rural areas. Almost 8½ percent of Ulster's housing was found to be unfit, compared to 5½ percent in England. [14]

Some of the worst housing conditions in Ulster are found in the government-run housing projects in Belfast and (London)Derry. Like so much else in Northern Ireland, these publicly owned buildings tend to be segregated by religion. Those in loyalist neighborhoods are inhabited almost entirely by Protestants. Those in nationalist neighborhoods—like Falls Road or the Bogside slum in (London)Derry—are inhabited by Catholics.

Although the buildings are similar in structure, the loyalist-run councils keep the buildings in loyalist neighborhoods in much better repair. [15] The roofs of the buildings in Catholic neighborhoods often leak in Ulster's drizzly weather. Some of the tiny apartments have no electricity, and many have no central heating. [16] The lack of heat can be fatal in Ulster's cold winters. An activist group calling itself The Right to

These children are playing in the housing project where they live. Ireland's children have been hit hard by the continuing strife and violence in the country.

Fuel claims that over eight hundred residents of Ulster die from the cold each year.[17]

Ironically, one place the government claims that housing conditions are not overcrowded is in Northern Ireland's prisons. There are no less than six prisons in the province, four of which have been built since 1970.[18]

The generally peaceable nature of Ulster's population is even reflected in its prisons. No prisoner has been killed, either by a fellow prisoner or by a guard, for more than fourteen years. Prison guards and other staff members do not carry weapons on the job, and there is little if any problem with drugs or with AIDS inside the prisons.[19]

6

RELIGION, POLITICS, AND POWER IN NORTHERN IRELAND

Northern Ireland has the highest proportion of church-goers in the United Kingdom. Four out of five people in Ulster belong to either a Protestant or a Catholic congregation, compared to only one in six in Great Britain.[1] This being so, one might think that Ulster would be a model of peace and goodwill. But instead, there seems to be some truth to the ironic saying that "Northern Ireland has too many Catholics, and twice as many Protestants, but not nearly enough Christians."[2]

It is impossible to talk about the struggle in Northern Ireland without talking in terms of Protestants and Catholics—or "Prods" and "Papists," as they sometimes call each other. They are on opposite sides of almost every political issue.

This often misleads people into thinking that the struggle in Northern Ireland is a religious conflict. It is not. Ulster's Protestants and Catholics are not fighting over religion. They are not arguing over different views of God or different interpretations of the New Testament. They are fighting over power. Each side wants to control the homeland it considers rightfully its own.

The tendency to confuse religion with power politics has a long history in Ireland. As far back as the seventeenth century, when Protestant and Catholic rulers were struggling for control of the British throne, Irish Catholics supported Charles I and James II mostly because they were Catholics and their opponents were not.

The Penal Laws were based on politics. They were designed to punish those who took the wrong side in Britain's power struggle. But most of those were Catholics, and the Penal Laws were aimed as much at the Catholic church and its practices as at individual Irish rebels.

Monks, bishops, and archbishops were forbidden to hold religious services, even in private. Presumably, the authorities were afraid that such services would turn into political meetings. Only lowly parish priests were allowed to celebrate the Catholic mass, and only in private, *and* after getting local government permission. Suffering from this kind of governmental persecution of their religion, it is hardly surprising that Catholics began to associate devotion to their church with their resentment of the Protestant-dominated government.

By the early nineteenth century, the divisions between the Protestants and Catholics had become even deeper. But those divisions were still more economic and political than religious. As farm laborers working for Presbyterian tenants on land owned by Anglo-Irish landlords, the Catholics were at the bottom of the economic heap. While living conditions for the Presbyterian tenants were hard, those of the Catholics were often desperate.

Once Catholics became able to bid to become tenants, the competition between them and the Presbyterians became intense. Daniel O'Connell's Catholic emancipation movement added a strong element of political tension to the competition that already existed. The Presbyterians began to fear the growing political power of the Catholic majority. More and more, they looked to their fellow Protestants—the Anglo-Irish and the British monarchy—for protection. Soon they, too, came to identify their political interests with their religious interests.

For most of the past several hundred years, most church leaders have done little to clear up the confusion between politics and religion. Father Murphy, who led the Wexford rebellion, was a priest. There were priests who fought with the IRA in the early twentieth century, and many more who helped and protected its fighters. Although the Catholic church was officially neutral in the battle over home rule, it welcomed the prospect of a Catholic Ireland. And the Irish Republic, when it was finally established, passed laws that reflected the Catholic church's teachings on divorce and abortion.

By the same token, the leaders of the Protestant churches have always had ties to the powerful Orange Order. And the Orangemen have always supplied the leaders of the Unionist forces in Ulster. Ian Paisley himself is a Protestant cleric.

In all this confusion of religious and political interests, political values have tended to win out over religious ones. Both Catholic priests and Protestant ministers alike proclaim the Christian principles of love and charity toward their fellow human beings. Yet their flocks live in fear, hatred, and often violence toward each other.

THE CHURCHES AND VIOLENCE

Officially, all the Christian churches—and most of the church leaders—condemn the violence in Northern Ireland. And yet, there is a feeling among many churchgoers, Protestant and Catholic alike, that the condemnation is not entirely heartfelt.

The proclamations of many religious leaders tend to reinforce this feeling, in the sense that such proclamations are usually highly colored by leaders' political views. As Sister Anna, an Episcopalian nun working for integrated education in Ulster, explains: Catholic officials "tend to pick up any complaints that the [Catholic] minority might have." This view reinforces the sense that the IRA is justified in its outrage, even if its methods are too extreme. Presbyterian leaders, on the other hand, tend to be "very keen on law and order." This insistence tends to support the actions of the British troops, and even of the Protestant paramilitary groups who claim to be fighting for the protection of the established order. And Church of Ireland leaders, Sister Anna adds, tend to be "slightly feeble about everything."3 This description of the attitudes of many church leaders is borne out by their public statements.

The extremists on both sides seem to see no contradiction between their Christian religious beliefs and the terrorism they support. The ties between many Catholics and the IRA are a prime example of the twisted relationship between religion and politics in Ulster.

The IRA claims to speak for the Catholic community. Yet it is very far from being a Catholic organization. It agrees with the Protestants that the Catholic church is much too powerful in the Republic. The united Ireland it looks forward to is a left-wing, secular (nonreligious) state. Alex Maskey, a member of the IRA-based Workers Party, insists that the IRA is "obviously in favor of freedom for religion."[4] By that he means that it is not Catholic in its positions. Less sympathetic observers would put it differently. They would argue that the IRA is, in fact, against *all* religion.

And yet, the IRA draws most of its members from the Catholic neighborhoods. Many individual priests are openly sympathetic to the IRA and even to the Provos. Many have helped the IRA in the past, and some are helping it today. At least one Irish priest is wanted in England to face charges of supplying the Provos with weapons to carry out terrorist attacks. And when Provos are killed committing such activities, they are usually buried in the IRA section of the Catholic Milltown Cemetery in Andersonstown, with a priest officiating at the funeral mass.

A similar relationship exists between the Protestant terrorist groups and some Presbyterian congregations, particularly the Free Presbyterian Church founded by the Reverend Ian Paisley.

TRIBES

If the conflict in Northern Ireland is not religious, why then does it divide so neatly along Catholic-Protestant lines? The answer seems to lie in the nature of Ulster society. The clue to that nature—like the clue to everything else in modern Ulster—lies in the distant past.

When the Celts started coming across the Irish Sea three thousand years ago, they came in tribes. And they kept their tribal identification after they got there. Ulster itself was originally a tribal kingdom. Its forests and fields were tribal lands.

As we have seen, the Celts prided themselves on being warriors. The tribes often fought among themselves, sometimes in alliance with other tribes and sometimes individually. After hundreds, and finally thousands of years, the different tribes became very similar to each other. But they clung to their tribal identities as long as they could.

In a sense, the people of Ulster are still tribal today. To an outsider, they seem almost identical. Ironically, Ulster's Protestants are closer to Ulster's Catholics—in moral, social, and cultural beliefs and attitudes—than they are to either the British or to their Irish neighbors in the south.[5] And yet, they divide themselves into warring groups—like the ancient Celtic tribes.

Religion is one way—practically the only way—that the modern tribes in Ulster can define themselves. Church services in Northern Ireland are not only religious rites. They are tribal rituals as well. "Protestant" and "Catholic" are not really religious terms at all; they are cultural descriptions.

"To be a 'Catholic' or a 'Protestant' in Northern Ireland is to be baptized into a certain closed way of life," as Lynne Shivers and David Bowman say in their book *More Than the Troubles*. "The nearest example for most Americans is the racial grouping in our cities, based on color. [But] in Northern Ireland, color is not the factor, *history* is. To be 'Protestant' or 'Catholic' means to accept a view of oneself, one's family, one's neighborhood, one's context within a closed group, that gives identity."[6]

According to a 1988 study, this "tribal loyalty transcends every consideration" in Ulster.[7] Each of the tribes—the Protestant and the Catholic—clings desperately to its own identity and to the hostility and fear it feels toward its neighbors. Only these days, the neighbors are not the members of the tribe across the river but the Papists or the Prods on the other side of the peace line.

EVEN DOGS AND ATHEISTS

In a tribal society like Northern Ireland, the worst thing is to be without a tribe. To have no tribe is to be an outsider, an outcast, without a place in the world. Because of this, almost everyone in Northern Ireland belongs to one tribe or the other. Everyone is a Protestant or a Catholic, whether he or she is religious or not. As author Richard Rose has written, "Even an atheist must be a Catholic or a Protestant atheist."[8]

And more than people are identified by religion in Ulster, as one man found out when he rushed to a Belfast hospital after being bitten by a dog. The first question the emergency room doctor asked him was not how big the dog was, or whether it seemed to be rabid. Instead the doctor asked him, "Was it a Catholic dog or a Protestant dog?"[9]

POLITICAL PARTIES

There are six major political parties in Northern Ireland and several smaller ones. Since Ulster has no national or provincial government of its own, the parties campaign for the twelve Ulster seats in the British House of Commons and for places on the councils that govern Ulster at the local level. These local councils exercise much of the economic and political power in Northern Ireland. They control the assignments to public housing, as well as the awarding of public jobs, which make up over 40 percent of all the jobs in the province.

Three of the major parties are unionist/loyalist. The largest is the Official Unionist Party (also known as the OUP, the Ulster Unionists, or simply the Unionists), which has been the biggest party in Ulster since the time of partition. An even more hard-line loyalist party is the Democratic Unionist Party (or DUP). Founded by Ian Paisley, it represents those Protestants who feel that the OUP is too moderate to speak for them. Much more to the unionist center is the Alliance Party. Founded in 1970, it tries to appeal not just to Protestants but also to those Catholics who feel that some tie with Britain is inevitable. Essentially a force for compromise, it has not flourished in Ulster's bitterly divided atmosphere.

On the other side of the peace lines, the Social Democratic and Labor Party (or SDLP) represents most of Ulster's Catholics. It calls for an eventual peaceful reunion with the Republic of Ireland.

Also nationalist, but much more radical, is Sinn Fein, Ulster's branch of the party that led the fight for Irish independence in the early twentieth century. Sinn Fein is really less a political party, however, than the public arm of the outlawed IRA. Although its president, Gerry Adams, was elected to the British Parliament from a heavily Catholic area in West Belfast, he refuses to attend its sessions.

Among the smaller parties are two that demonstrate, once again, the two-sidedness of nearly everything in Northern Ireland. The Workers Party and the Ulster Loyalist Democratic Party (or ULDP) are both socialist in their programs. But the Workers Party is an outgrowth of the old Official Wing of the IRA,[10] while the ULDP grew out of the loyalist Ulster Defence Association.

In the 1989 elections, which chose the members of

the local councils for the next four years, the OUP won about 35 percent of all the seats across the province. The extreme loyalist DUP won a little less than 20 percent, as did the moderate nationalist SDLP. The Alliance Party took only 7 percent. The remaining seats were won by members of the various smaller parties or independents.[11]

THE ORANGE ORDER

The political parties are not the only sources of political power in Northern Ireland. In a way, they are not even the most important ones. Many Irishmen believe that the Orange Order holds most of the real political power in Ulster, and always has.

As we have seen, the Orange Order is a secret society named for William of Orange, the Protestant English king who defeated the Catholics in the Battle of the Boyne over three hundred years ago. It is closely tied to the OUP. The two organizations share many of the same leaders. For most Orangemen, it is probably true that their strongest loyalty is to the Order, rather than to the party.

In his book *Northern Ireland: Captive of History*, the Irish journalist Gary MacEoin described the society's power this way: "The role of the Orange Order in Northern Ireland since the founding of the state has been very similar to the role of the Communist Party in the Soviet Union. Although not officially a part of the system of government, it dominated the executive, the legislative and the judicial branches. Only its members could hope to gain office, and they showed their appreciation openly by carrying out the policies it formulated."[12]

Blackmen, as the leaders of the Orange Order are

*Every July 12, Orangemen march in their bowler
hats and white gloves to celebrate the victory
of Protestant King William of Orange over Catholic
King James II at the Battle of the Boyne in 1690.
The parades generally go through Catholic neighborhoods and are often marked by violence.*

known, have always dominated the Unionist Party. Through it, they dominated Stormont, as they still dominate many of Ulster's local councils. If anything, the loyalist politicians on these local councils are even more likely to be tied to the Orange Order—and to be fiercely anti-Catholic—than are the politicians at the provincial level.

THE POWER OF THE GUN

There is, of course, another kind of power in Northern Ireland: the brute power of the gun and the bomb. This is the power exercised by the terrorists on both sides of the peace lines.

The terrorists' power is basically destructive. It is the power of the veto. It can destroy any attempt to find a political settlement, but it cannot achieve a political settlement itself. It cannot build a positive future. What it can do is to create chaos in the present. And, for the past two decades, that is just what the terrorists in Ulster have done.

7

THE TERRORISTS

Northern Ireland has many problems. They include deep-seated tribal/religious divisions, seemingly unsolvable political conflicts, and widespread unemployment and poverty. But none of Ulster's problems is greater than the terrorism that stalks the province.

In 1988 (the last year for which there are statistics), there were 358 shootings and 253 bombings by terrorists in Ulster. In addition, 205 more bombs were found before they could explode. In all 93 men, women, and children were killed, and 1,047 were injured. [1]

Terrorism in Northern Ireland is not just a problem in itself. It makes each of Ulster's other problems worse. It inflames religious hatreds. It hardens political attitudes. And it discourages the business investment that might save Northern Ireland's failing economy.

WHAT IS TERRORISM?

Terrorism is the use of violence and the threat of violence to achieve political ends. Terrorists attempt to

Another hearse carrying another victim of Northern Ireland's terrorist attacks. This particular person was killed, along with ten others, when a bomb exploded in a community center in Enniskillen, Northern Ireland.

frighten whole societies into doing what they want. Since the terrorists' aim is to promote fear, their crimes are usually especially brutal and horrifying. They often involve violence against civilians.[2]

Many individuals, as well as revolutionary and criminal groups—and even governments—use terrorism. But few groups admit that they are terrorists. They usually call themselves paramilitary groups or private armies.

It is sometimes said that "one person's terrorist is another person's freedom fighter, and vice versa." This means that most people only use the word to describe groups whose goals they oppose. They consider those who use the same tactics to fight for causes they support as guerrilla fighters—and even heroes. This is the case in Northern Ireland, where powerful groups on both the nationalist and unionist sides have turned to terror.

The use of violence and fear to gain political ends is an old tradition in Ireland. The powerful Orange Order, the oldest and largest of the Protestant secret societies, was founded in the 1790s, when Catholic farmers first started to bid against Protestant farmers to become tenants on the same farmlands. The Orangemen used terrorist methods to frighten the Catholics from bidding for the tenancies.[3] The Peep-O-Day Boys were essentially terrorists who worked for the landlords. They got their name by breaking into Catholic homes early in the morning, while the families were asleep, supposedly to search for weapons.

About the same time, several smaller Catholic secret societies, including the Whiteboys and the Defenders, were formed to strike out against the English landlords. Before long, much of the Irish countryside was being terrorized by one side or the other—or both. Violence escalated.

Ulster is still being terrorized by both sides today.

NATIONALIST TERRORISTS

The Provos of the IRA are the best-known "paramilitary" group in Ulster. Following the partition of Ireland in the 1920s, the IRA continued to hope that it could force the reunion of Ireland. But after the civil war, the energy ran out of the movement. The IRA lost much of its support on both sides of the border.

The Catholic civil rights movement of the late 1960s—and the violent Protestant response to it—brought some of the spirit back into the nationalists' demand for a united Ireland.

A split developed over strategy within the IRA itself. One branch wanted to work openly and relatively peacefully, not only for reunion but for the development of a socialist, nonreligious Irish state. The other branch of the IRA wanted to wage a virtual war, using terrorist tactics, against the British and their supporters in Ulster.

Instead of going one way or the other, the IRA went in both directions at once. It divided into two separate organizations. The Provisional Wing of the IRA—the Provos—is the group directly responsible for most of the violence for which the IRA is known. The Official Wing of the IRA, on the other hand, denies participation in the violence. In recent years, the Official IRA has been all but silent. Its place as the public defender of the Provos and as the political arm of the fight against the British has been taken by Sinn Fein.

British officials claim the separation between the

IRA and Sinn Fein is artificial. They argue that it is only a handy lie that allows Sinn Fein to campaign and raise money openly, despite the fact that the Provisionals have been outlawed as a terrorist organization.

When asked why Parliament does not simply outlaw Sinn Fein as well, a British official admitted it was because the government has "no evidence of their terrorist connections or actions."4 Even so, the British are convinced that those connections—and actions—exist.

In any case, both the IRA and Sinn Fein are working toward the same ends. The stated goals of both involve not only driving the British out of Ulster, but establishing a secular (that is, nonreligious) and socialist government for all of Ireland.

The ends of the IRA are less important to most residents of Ulster than the means the Provos use to reach them. As we have already seen, those means commonly include bombings, shootings, and political assassinations.

IRA strategy in the past involved the use of random violence, including car bombs left in public places that indiscriminately killed anyone who happened to be nearby. These days, however, the IRA claims that it has given up random violence. It insists that it is fighting a war against a foreign military force that is occupying Ireland. Instead of carrying out general terrorism against the population, it says it attacks only British soldiers and officials, and those it sees as traitors who support them.5

There is some truth to their claim. In recent years, most IRA attacks have been aimed at targets that have some direct relation to the British army, the British government, or the Royal Ulster Constabulary. (The IRA considers members of the RUC to be collaborators with the British enemy.) Those targets have included

Masked IRA gunmen fire a volley of shots in West Belfast in honor of an IRA sniper who was shot by British troops.

British soldiers, both inside Ulster and in England, and RUC members, whether on- or off-duty. They have also included officials of the British government. It was the IRA that tried to assassinate British prime minister Margaret Thatcher in 1984, and that did murder Earl Louis Mountbatten in 1979. In addition, the IRA keeps up a constant campaign of sabotage against the railroad lines linking Northern Ireland and the Republic. The line between Belfast and Dublin was cut at least forty times in the first four months of 1989 alone.[6]

This does not mean that the IRA has stopped killing and injuring civilians. It hasn't. Some of the people killed have been accused of betraying the IRA in some fashion. Most, however, have been killed by what the IRA calls "mistakes." On April 12, 1989, for example, an IRA bomb killed a young woman and wounded thirty other people in the seaside town of Warrenpoint. The bomb was intended to destroy a nearby RUC station.

The next day, the IRA announced that it had intended to issue a warning before the bomb went off so that civilians could leave the area. The bomb had gone off fifteen minutes early by accident. "We offer our sincerest apologies to those bereaved and injured,"[7] it said.

Such "mistakes" are extremely common. As John Hermon, an ex-head of the RUC, has declared: "[T]he IRA has shown time and time again that their 'mistakes' in killing and maiming civilians are an inevitable, unavoidable part of their campaign. They know it—and their apologies and explanations are fraudulent."[8] In any case, it seems clear that the Provos are either unconcerned with civilian lives or helpless to carry out their attacks without taking them "by mistake."

The IRA is not the only nationalist group that uses terror. The smaller and even more radical Irish National Liberation Army has carried out many bombings and killings of its own. It, too, is committed to a united and socialist Ireland.

UNIONIST TERRORISTS

Although the IRA gets most of the world's attention, the Protestants have many terrorists of their own. In fact, as *Maclean's* magazine has pointed out: "The first people killed in the current troubles were Catholics gunned down by Loyalists. The first bombs that exploded in Ulster in 1969 were Protestant bombs. And the first policeman shot to death in 1970 was killed by Unionist extremists."[9]

With about six thousand members, the Ulster Defence Association (or UDA) is the largest of the loyalist paramilitary groups. In addition to its own activities, the UDA is widely believed to be the power behind the much smaller secret organization known as the Ulster Freedom Fighters (or UFF). The UFF is noted for its many murders of Catholic civilians and for its bombings of Catholic schools and other Catholic institutions.[10] Together with another Protestant terrorist group called the Red Hand Commandos, the Ulster Freedom Fighters were outlawed for terrorism in 1973.[11]

The UDA itself, however, remains a legal organization. Although the government is aware of the UDA role in Protestant violence, it takes the position that belonging to the UDA does not, by itself, make someone a terrorist.

The UDA was begun about 1971 by street gangs in

Although the Catholic IRA has gotten most of the attention and publicity in Northern Ireland, there are Protestant terrorist groups as well. This Catholic boy stands in front of his family's shop, which was destroyed by Protestant paramilitaries.

the Protestant Shankill Road neighborhood of Belfast. They organized as vigilantes, supposedly to protect their neighborhoods from the IRA. At that time, the UFF's forerunners won their nickname of the "Shankill Butchers" by slitting the throats of unfortunate Catholics. [12]

Like all the other loyalist groups, the UDA wants Northern Ireland to stay within the United Kingdom. If that is not possible, however, it wants an independent Ulster—run, of course, by the Protestant majority.

The UDA was strongly opposed to direct rule when it was first imposed in 1972. It saw direct rule as a scheme to undermine Protestant control. For a time, UDA paramilitaries even clashed with British troops over the issue. But the real targets of the UDA remain Ulster's Catholics, whom they see as the real enemy.

Another group, known as the Ulster Volunteer Force (or UVF), carries on in the name of the old Ulster Volunteers, who fought home rule in the early twentieth century. It burst on the scene in 1966, when it "declared war" on the IRA, despite the fact that the IRA had been inactive for many years at that time. [13]

The UVF proceeded to launch an extensive campaign of sabotage and assassination, apparently aimed at disrupting talks between the prime ministers of Northern Ireland and the Republic. Condemned by Ulster's then Prime Minister, Terence O'Neill, the UVF was outlawed and several of its leaders were thrown in jail.

The UVF was not completely destroyed, however, as was proven on a quiet Sunday afternoon in the spring of 1988. On that day, two members of the UVF walked into the Avenue Bar in a poor area of Belfast. There were about twenty customers in the small neighborhood pub, most of them Catholic workers who lived in the area. One of the terrorists took a submachine gun from under his coat and opened fire on them. Three were killed, and ten others were wounded.[14]

The terrorists of the UDA and the UVF make no distinction between supporters of the IRA and other Catholics. For them, all Catholics are IRA sympathizers. All Catholics are equally guilty. Therefore, while some of the loyalists' victims have ties to the IRA, many others do not. In July 1989, for example, a Catholic coal worker named John Devine was murdered in his own home by Protestant gunmen. The killers simply walked in through his unlocked front door and shot him down in front of his thirteen-year-old son. Devine had no known political ties. The only reason for him to be killed was that he lived in a heavily Catholic neighborhood in West Belfast.

As Roman Catholic bishop Cahal Daly declared at Devine's funeral: "It would seem as though any Catholic in that street would have been seen by [the terrorists] as a target for murder, and that John's was the first house to which they came with its door open."[15]

SUPPORT FOR THE TERRORISTS

The number of people who actually take part in the murders and the bombings is relatively small. The IRA, for example, has only about fifty members who plan and run its operations, and possibly some two hundred more on what it calls "active service."[16] The UVF, too, is estimated to have between two hundred and three hundred active members.[17] But each of the major terrorist groups receives a great deal of sympathy and support from within its community as well.

Members of "Ulster's Third Force for God and Ulster" gather for a "parade of force." This group has been described as existing to counteract IRA terrorism and to protect the Protestant people.

There are many Protestants who feel that the UDA, the UFF, the UVF, and the rest, protect them by keeping the Catholics in line; many Catholics feel that the IRA is fighting for their freedom. Because of feelings like these, many people who would never take part in killings themselves give help and protection to those who do.

Some help directly, by contributing money to a terrorist group or by hiding its members or weapons from the police. Sometimes the help is indirect or even passive. It is a rare Protestant witness to a UVF attack who would identify the criminal to the police, and a rare Catholic who would turn in a member of the IRA. Without such protection, the terrorists could not act nearly as openly and as effectively as they do.

Still, it is hard to tell just how widespread willing support for the terrorists actually is. The terrorists themselves would probably argue that almost all their fellow religionists support them in their hearts. The British government, on the other hand, claims that what seems like wide community support is really the result of fear and intimidation. Certainly some of it is. People who betray terrorists may be killed or at least kneecapped. ("Kneecapping" means shooting someone in the knee, shattering the kneecap and often permanently crippling the victim. It is a common means of punishment among terrorists in Northern Ireland.)

Both the government and the terrorists overstate their case. Willing support for the terrorists is not nearly as widespread as they claim. But it is there, and it is real. One indication of how widespread support is may be the turnout at such terrorist rituals as funerals. Although there are probably only about 250 active IRA terrorists in Ulster, some 10,000 Catholic mourners showed up at the Milltown cemetery for the funeral of the three killed in Gibraltar.[18]

FUNDING THE TERROR

Both the UDA and the IRA fund their activities through a combination of donations from sympathizers, profits from legal and illegal businesses, armed robberies, smuggling, and other criminal enterprises.

The businesses include hotels, drinking clubs, and gambling machines in the neighborhoods. The criminal enterprises include widespread extortion. In 1988 alone, police suspected that 653 robberies were connected to the terrorists on one side or the other, with a total take of more than 1 million pounds (roughly $1.5 million).[19] That may have been small compared to the terrorists' profits from what is known as the protection racket. The terrorists force the owners of small businesses to pay them money for "protection," or else see their businesses destroyed. In February 1989, the UDA's commander for South Belfast, Jackie MacDonald, was formally charged with running an extortion scheme at Belfast building sites.[20]

Individual terrorists on both sides have been accused of corruption—of using funds collected for their organizations for their own purposes. The UDA, in particular, seems to have a large proportion of out-and-out crooks on its rolls. The terrorists police themselves to some extent, and several members of both the IRA and the UDA have been kneecapped or murdered for stealing from their own organizations.

Ironically, the terrorists sometimes function as a vigilante police force of a kind. In several of the more violent and heavily segregated neighborhoods, the official police are ineffective at best. In those neighborhoods, it is the paramilitaries who keep the ordinary muggers and petty crooks in line. As an SDLP council member from Belfast complained, "When the police are not seen to take action against [the criminals], the people welcome action by the paramilitaries. . . ."[21]

Both sides have large stockpiles of weapons hidden away. The IRA's stockpiles are intended for use in the current struggle. But the UDA and the other Protestant terrorists also have a more distant future in mind. They are hoarding weapons against the chance that the British will one day abandon them to a Catholic-dominated Ireland. When and if that day comes, they are determined to be ready to fight for Ulster's independence.

The weapons range from ordinary pistols to submachine guns, and from dynamite to ultramodern Czechoslovakian Semtex explosives. No one can know for sure just how many guns and bombs are squirreled away around the province, but in 1988 alone, security forces found 10,425 pounds of explosives, 552 firearms, and over 100,000 rounds of ammunition in various hiding places.[22] In September 1988, police found a loyalist "gun factory" turning out Uzi-like submachine guns in Ballynahinch near Belfast.[23] In January 1989, they uncovered an IRA "bomb factory" in a house in a residential neighborhood in (London)Derry. Finds like those are probably little more than tips of some very large and deadly icebergs.

Even more worrisome to the authorities is the suspicion that the terrorists are starting to stockpile sophisticated missiles, like the Soviet-built SA-7 and the American-built Stinger, which could be used to shoot down aircraft.[24]

FOREIGN CONNECTIONS

Paramilitaries on both sides have connections with foreign groups or governments, from whom they obtain at least some of their weapons and support.

The loyalists' main relationship seems to be with South Africa. A recent scandal embarrassed not only the Protestants and the government of South Africa, but the British government as well.

According to news reports in Ireland and elsewhere,[25] loyalist paramilitaries were told in 1985 that the South African government was willing to deal for weapons. They sent an agent to South Africa to check out the weapons. When he protested at the high prices asked for them, the South Africans offered a different kind of deal. The weapons could be traded for something even more valuable—secrets about military missiles that the Short Brothers electronics firm was manufacturing in Northern Ireland for the British government.

The scandal hit the press when three men tied to the UDA and a group called the Ulster Resistance were arrested in Paris, France. An official from the South African embassy in Paris was arrested with them. The men had parts from a Shorts-built missile system with them at the time and were apparently negotiating to sell them to the South African.

The revelation of possible ties between the UDA and South Africa were disturbing to the British government. But the foreign connections of the IRA are even more disturbing—and considerably more extensive.

The IRA is a leading member of a network of prominent left-wing terrorist organizations that have, at one time or another, included the Palestinian Fatah, the German Red Brigades, and the Japanese Army of the

Red Star. These groups all tend to find their weapons, money, and other support from each other, and from certain friendly governments.[26] One of the most important of those governments in recent years was that of Muammar Qaddafi. Sworn to help "people's revolutions" around the world, the Libyan leader sent some 100 tons of weapons and explosives to the IRA between 1985 and 1986 alone. The onetime undersecretary of state for Northern Ireland, Tom King, accused Qaddafi of supplying IRA members the weapons they used in their most recent wave of terror in 1989.[27]

But the strongest—and most profitable—of the IRA's foreign ties are with descendants of Irish immigrants in the United States. Like so much else to do with Northern Ireland, these ties are reflections of the past.

When the Young Ireland movement was destroyed in 1848, many Young Irishmen fled to America. There, they founded the Fenian Movement to work for Irish independence. Fenian groups were started in both the United States and in Ireland itself. The American Fenians campaigned among the large Irish-American community to raise funds—and volunteers—to help the Fenians in Ireland. After the Civil War, American Fenians planned several invasions of British Canada. In 1867, the Fenians sailed a boat called *Erin's Hope*, filled with weapons and supplies, to Ireland. They were captured while trying to land.

Like the Young Irishmen, the Fenian Movement eventually died out. But its cause lived on in many of the Fenian's children, and in their children's children, in America. These Irish-Americans continue to donate to the old cause by giving money to the Irish Northern Aid Committee, better known as NORAID.

A huge arms cache seized in New York City in 1983.
Eight men were charged with conspiring to sell more
than $2 billion worth of arms to, among other groups
and countries, the Irish Republican Army.

Many Americans, like these people at a St. Patrick's Day parade in Detroit, Michigan, feel very strongly about the situation in Ireland.

The British government insists that the money they give helps fund IRA terrorism in Ulster. There is no question that NORAID has close ties to the IRA. In April 1981, a U.S. court ruled that NORAID was, in fact, an agent of the Provisional Wing of the IRA.[28] But NORAID claims that the money from America goes primarily to support the widows and orphans of Catholics killed in the Troubles, and not to support the political or paramilitary activities of the IRA.

CRACKING DOWN ON TERROR

Ever since the current Troubles began, the British government has been taking increasingly drastic measures to fight the terrorists. Some of these measures are extremely controversial, because they violate rights and protections traditionally granted to all British citizens.

These violations have been made legal by a series of supposedly "emergency" or "temporary" laws. The most important of these are: the Northern Ireland (Emergency Provisions) Acts of 1978 and 1987 and the Prevention of Terrorism (Emergency Provisions) Act of 1984. The Prevention of Terrorism Act was made permanent in 1989.[29]

These laws allow the government to ban anyone it suspects of "involvement" in terrorism from the United Kingdom. In addition, the security forces are allowed to search citizens' homes and other property merely on "suspicion," and to hold people in jail for up to seven days without bringing them before a court or allowing them to seek legal advice. Many prisoners held under these conditions complain of bad treatment from the police. One thirteen-year-old boy had his confession to murdering a policeman thrown out because he had been grilled for fifteen hours—most of the time in his underwear—before being allowed to see either an attorney or his family.[30] Other prisoners have complained of verbal threats and even of beatings.

Suspects accused of terrorist activities are denied the traditional British right to a trial by jury. Instead, they are tried in what are called "Diplock courts." In these courts, cases are heard by a single judge. The government argues that Diplock courts are necessary because it would be too easy for terrorists to intimidate members of a jury.

Another right denied to suspected terrorists is the historic right to silence. Traditionally, as in the United States, British defendants have the right to remain silent. Courts are forbidden to let that silence prejudice them against the defendant. But now, the British government has ordered that a suspected terrorist's silence can be used against him or her at trial.[31]

In 1988, the British government imposed a special form of censorship on the television and radio news media of the United Kingdom. It is now illegal for the media to broadcast the actual voice, whether live or taped, of anyone the government claims supports terrorism. In practice, this has meant anyone who supports the IRA. The ban even includes the voice of Gerry Adams, who is not only the leader of a legal political party (Sinn Fein), but a duly elected member of the British Parliament as well.

CONCERN OVER HUMAN RIGHTS

Measures like these have aroused storms of protest, both inside and outside Ulster. The British government dismisses most of the homegrown protests, claiming that they come almost entirely from members of the

Catholic community who are sympathetic to the terrorists and their activities.

But some of the outside protests are harder for the government to ignore. The internationally respected human rights group, Amnesty International, has expressed concern to the British government over several of its practices. Among them are the procedures of the Diplock courts. According to Amnesty International, many convictions in these courts have been based almost entirely on the testimony of "supergrasses"— suspects who point the finger at others in return for lighter sentences for themselves.[32] Over half of the paramilitaries (nationalist and loyalist alike) convicted between 1983 and 1985 were convicted on this kind of evidence. All but one (sixty-four out of sixty-five) were later released on appeal.[33] Even some of Ulster's own judges have protested against the changes in a prisoner's right to silence and the government's practice of holding suspects for long periods of time without bringing charges against them.[34] And the deputy leader of Britain's opposition Labour Party, Ray Hattersley, has called the entire Prevention of Terrorism Act "deeply offensive to civil rights."[35]

The International Federation of Journalists, which represents some 150,000 journalists around the world, has protested Britain's "systematic and extensive" attempt to muzzle press freedom in Northern Ireland. In addition to the ban on voices sympathetic to the terrorists, the federation is concerned about recent changes in Britain's Official Secrets Act. It claims the changes give the government the right to jail journalists without proving that they have done anything to hurt the public interest.[36]

Most telling of all, the International Court of Human Rights has ruled against Britain twelve different times for violating rights in Northern Ireland. That's more than it has ruled against any other European country.[37]

British Prime Minister Margaret Thatcher admits that some of the security measures "do restrict freedom." But, she adds, "Those who live by the bomb and the gun, and those who support them, can't in all circumstances be accorded exactly the same rights as everyone else."[38]

SHOOT TO KILL?

The most controversial of all human rights issues in Ulster centers around the IRA's claim that the security forces are operating on a "shoot-to-kill" basis. That is, that they have a policy of shooting IRA agents on sight, without giving them a chance to surrender. Sinn Fein insists that this "shoot-to-kill" policy began in 1970 and continues to this day.

In 1982, the British government appointed a retired British policeman named John Stalker to find out if security officials in Ulster had such a policy. Specifically, he was asked to look into three separate incidents in which six unarmed men had been killed. Stalker later complained that members of the RUC had prevented him from carrying out his investigation. Stalker was eventually removed from the case by the government in London. A later investigation, carried out by the chief constable for Staffordshire, Charles Kelly, found no policy as such but recommended disciplinary hearings for twenty-two officers of the RUC.[39]

The government still denies that it ever had, or even tolerated, a shoot-to-kill policy. Still, the fact remains that several unarmed people—most, but not all, associated with the IRA—have been killed by security forces. And, on the rare occasions anyone has been punished for the killings, the punishment has usually been light.

A notable exception was made in 1984, when a single British soldier was sentenced to life in prison for shooting down a demonstrator. But even that punishment failed to stick. The soldier was released in 1988. Many Catholics were outraged when he was immediately reinstated in the British army.[40]

The gunning down of the three unarmed IRA agents in Gibraltar in 1988 reawakened many Catholics' belief that a shoot-to-kill policy still exists. When the British agents who did the shooting were cleared of any wrongdoing, many Catholics felt that belief had been confirmed.

8

THE SEARCH FOR PEACE

As we have seen in earlier chapters, the Troubles in Northern Ireland have been going on for a long time, and they show no sign of ending. The terrorists on both sides have stockpiles of weapons that suggest a long, long fight ahead.

The whole generation of young adults who live in Ulster today grew up with the Troubles. They cannot remember a time when British troops did not patrol the streets of their neighborhoods. They cannot remember a time when funerals of neighbors and friends killed in the Troubles were not regular occasions in their lives. And now many of them are having children of their own—children who will grow up in the same patrolled streets, attending the same funerals.

On a day-to-day basis, it often seems that all the news from Ulster is bad. Poverty, hatred, bombings, assassinations, riots, and kneecappings are all we hear about. There is no question that the situation is grim. It is sometimes hard to imagine that a real and lasting peace can ever come to such a troubled society.

If peace does come, it will have to be built on the foundation of a society that satisfies both the Protestant and Catholic communities. The people of each community must be convinced that the society in which they live is just and free, and fair to them. The day when that kind of society will exist in Ulster is a long way off. Yet steps are being taken even now to bring it closer—to build the kind of society in which both communities can live in peace and mutual respect.

Those steps include efforts to improve social justice, to encourage tolerance and understanding between Protestants and Catholics, and to promote economic development in the province.

GOVERNMENT EFFORTS

The British government has taken a number of positive steps to improve civil and human rights for Catholics in Northern Ireland. It is no longer illegal to fly the flag of the Republic in the north. The arrest powers of the Royal Ulster Constabulary have been somewhat limited, and the amount of time that suspects can be held in jail without being charged has been reduced.

These are only small changes. But the government insists that they are important signals to the Catholic community that it wants to improve the situation as soon as the violence quiets down enough to make it possible.

In the economic field, the government has made major changes in the province's employment laws. The 1976 Fair Employment Act forbade religious or political discrimination in hiring and set up a Fair Employment Agency to handle complaints. But after a decade in which Catholic unemployment only got worse, the government introduced a much stricter Fair Employment Bill in 1988.

It replaced the old and almost completely ineffective Fair Employment Agency with a more aggressive Fair Employment Commission. All businesses with more than ten employees now have to register with the commission. Each year, they must report how many Protestants and how many Catholics they employ. If these reports show discrimination, the commission can order them to correct their hiring practices. Employers who refuse to cooperate with the commission will be subject to both civil and criminal penalties. [1]

THE INTERNATIONAL FUND
FOR IRELAND

At the same time that Britain and the Republic established the Anglo-Irish Agreement in 1985, they set up the so-called International Fund for Ireland. The purpose of the fund is "to promote economic and social advance and to encourage contact, dialogue and reconciliation between nationalists and unionists throughout Ireland." That is, throughout *both* Irelands.

The fund attempts to do this by raising money from friendly governments and spending it to promote economic development. Three-quarters of the fund's money is spent in Northern Ireland. The rest goes to projects in the six counties of the Republic closest to the border with Northern Ireland—Louth, Monaghan, Cavan, Leitrim, Sligo, and Donegal.

The fund was launched in September 1986, with contributions from the United States, Canada, and New Zealand. Starting in 1988, the European Economic Community (or EEC), which is made up of several Western European countries, began contributing as well. The EEC has already assisted Ulster in other ways. In 1986–87, for example, two of the EEC's own funds contributed about $129 million to Northern Ireland.

All told, contributions and pledges to the International Fund total about $150 million. This is not a large amount of money in international financial terms. Still, the fund tries to multiply its economic effect by supporting projects that encourage increased private investment and promote the creation of new jobs in the economically depressed area.[2]

So far, outside businesses and governments have been slow to contribute to the fund. One reason may be the Troubles and the threat they present to a stable business atmosphere. At this time, the fund represents only a small step toward economic development in Northern Ireland. But it *is* a step. And it means that a mechanism is in place for other countries to help—if and when the parties within Ulster find a way to work together.

THE PEACE MOVEMENT

The real hope for peace in Northern Ireland will not come from small government steps toward greater freedom, or even from prosperity. It will come through people—individual people from both communities who are tired of the killing and who want to find ways to live in peace.

Although the terrorists and the politicians get most of the attention, many ordinary citizens in Northern Ireland are working every day to find ways to live together. They are searching desperately for ways to turn Ulster's long tragedy into a lasting peace.

One day in 1976, one of them, a young Catholic

woman named Betty Williams, was walking down a street in Belfast. Not far away, some children were playing. A car came hurtling around a corner, going much too fast and out of control. Williams watched in horror as the car rammed into the playing children. Three of them were killed.

It looked at first like a simple, though tragic, street accident. But as Betty Williams soon discovered, the children were three more victims of the Troubles. The driver of the runaway car turned out to be an IRA man who had been shot attempting to escape from British soldiers.

Like many of her neighbors in Belfast, Betty Williams was almost accustomed to the idea of innocent people—even children—being killed in the Troubles. But for her, these deaths were different. She had actually seen these children killed before her eyes. She could not simply accept their deaths and go on with her life as though nothing had happened. She had to do something to try to stop the slaughter that was taking place in her country.

What she did was to organize a march to protest the deaths of the children—to protest the seemingly endless cycle of violence and terror in Ulster. Some two hundred people participated in the march, which was held in Andersonstown, the center of IRA support in Belfast. It was brave of the marchers to take part. Protesting the IRA in a Catholic neighborhood of Belfast can be a dangerous thing to do.

One of the people who saw the march that day was another young Catholic woman named Mairead Corrigan. Corrigan was the aunt of the three children who had been killed. Filled with emotion, she joined the march. Later she sought out Betty Williams. Together, the two women talked about what else they might do to help end the terror.

Between them, they organized several more protest demonstrations designed to shame the consciences of both Catholics and Protestants alike. In the largest of these demonstrations, some thirty thousand people turned out for a single march. That represented almost one out of every ten residents of the entire city.

But the women did not stop with demonstrations. Knowing that much of the money—and many of the weapons—used by Irish terrorists comes from America, the two women traveled to the United States. They campaigned among the Irish-Americans who have traditionally supported the IRA, pleading with them not to send any more help to the terrorists in Ulster.

Their efforts did not end the violence in Northern Ireland, of course. But they made a difference. For more than a year, while the protests were at their height, there was a change in the atmosphere. Terrorist violence fell by one-half.[3] What is more, they were effective in cutting down the flow of supplies from America to the terrorists. And, perhaps most importantly of all, their organization is credited with saving the lives of at least 150 people who had been marked for death by the terrorists, by helping them to escape abroad.[4]

Williams and Corrigan received the 1976 Nobel Peace Prize for their efforts to bring peace and reconciliation to Northern Ireland. Eventually, the intensity of their efforts could not be kept up. The peace demonstrations ceased. But the women established an organization known as the Community of the Peace People, which today continues to work quietly toward peace and reconciliation.

It is not alone. There are several other organizations working in various ways toward the goal of peace in Northern Ireland.[5] Most of them are small, working within a single town or neighborhood. But taken together, they are having a real—if not yet measurable—effect on the thinking of many residents of Ulster.

Among these groups is Co-operation North, a private organization that works for greater understanding between the Protestant north and the Catholic Republic. With offices in both Belfast and Dublin, it encourages economic cooperation and promotes tourism and sporting competition between the two Irelands.

Several different groups promote "holiday schemes"—that is, vacation trips that give the children of the Troubles a chance to get away and find out what peace is really like. Some of these groups conduct holidays in the Irish countryside. Others, like Project Ulster and the Wisconsin Children's Program of Northern Ireland, bring children to the United States.

Many "schemes" mix Protestant and Catholic children together. For some of these children, it is the only chance they've ever had to meet a young person of the other community as a fellow human being. The organizers of such "schemes" hope that the friendships made on these holidays will one day help tear down the peace lines.

Both the Protestant and Catholic faiths have bodies that promote peace education in Northern Ireland schools. The Peace Education Programme of the Irish Council of Churches' Irish Commission for Justice and Peace represents the efforts of several Protestant churches, while the Irish Commission for Justice and Peace is an offshoot of the Roman Catholic Bishops' Conference.

Not everyone supports even these small steps

toward reconciliation. Father Sean McManus is the national director of the Irish National Caucus, a nationalist lobbying group based in Washington, D.C. When asked about the peace movement, Father McManus's answer was flat and absolute. "There is no peace movement in Northern Ireland,"[6] he insisted.

Father McManus believes that groups like the Community of the Peace People are little more than fronts, organized and probably paid for by the British government. For those who believe as Father McManus does, there can be no real peace in Ulster until the British are gone and Ireland is reunited.

INTEGRATED EDUCATION

The most hopeful of all the developments in Northern Ireland since the Troubles began is the growing movement toward integrated education.

Young people in Northern Ireland have to attend school until they are sixteen. For all that time, most students are segregated in schools attended only by members of their own community. Ulster's schools are not segregated by law. Parents are free to send their children to what we would call a public school or to a religious school, as they wish.

In practice, however, most Protestant parents send their children to public schools, and most Catholic parents send theirs to Catholic schools. (Ironically, this may be one area where Catholics have things better in Northern Ireland. Most observers believe that the quality of education tends to be somewhat higher in the Catholic schools.) Catholic priests and bishops have traditionally encouraged this segregation by insisting that Catholic children attend Catholic schools as a religious necessity.

In recent years, this rigid system of self-imposed segregation has begun to break down. The breakdown began in 1970 when two Catholic mothers decided to send their children to a public, or Protestant, grade school. They believed that the best hope for their children was to learn to live in peace—not in hate—with their Protestant neighbors.

In 1974, these mothers joined with a few Protestant parents to form a group they called All Children Together.[7] One of their hopes was to start an integrated Christian school, one that both Protestant and Catholic children could attend together.

All Children Together campaigned for and won the Westminster Education (Northern Ireland) Act of 1978 from the British Parliament. It allowed public schools that wanted to do so to become integrated. The law proved useless, however, because no existing school decided to switch.

Finally in the spring of 1981, some of the All Children Together parents were getting desperate. Their children were starting secondary school in the fall, and there was no integrated secondary school in the entire country. They decided to start one of their own.

At that time, All Children Together had only about $70 in the bank, but the parents went ahead with their plans anyway. The school opened on September 1, 1981, in a two-classroom building on a hill overlooking Belfast. It was named Lagan College, after the Lagan River, which runs through the city. That first year, the college had only twenty-eight students, all of them eleven years old, and two teachers.

According to Sister Anna, who helped the parents to found Lagan College, the policy from the start was that "there mustn't be any minorities in the school." Fourteen of those first twenty-eight students were

Protestant, fourteen were Catholic. Each of the two teachers came from each community.

This policy has been strictly maintained ever since. As much as possible, there has been an effort to integrate in other ways as well, with equal numbers of boys and girls, and rich and poor, and so on. According to Sister Anna, the school has been a great success. While not all the students get along, there have been no sectarian incidents in the school's history.

The enrollment has gone up in every year since 1981. Prefabricated mobile classrooms have been added as necessary. By 1984, Lagan had become large enough to receive a regular government educational grant. (Before then, it was supported entirely by voluntary contributions from parents and others who sympathized with its ideals.) Today, the school has about 550 students drawn from 60 elementary schools around Belfast, and receives about 85 percent of its funding from the government.

Three more integrated schools were started in 1985. One was another secondary school on the other side of Belfast. The other two, also in Belfast, were elementary schools. A fifth integrated school was started in the countryside in 1986, and two more (one in the northern part of the province and one in the south) in 1987. An eighth school opened in September 1988.

So far, only about two thousand students attend integrated schools. That's only about one-half of 1 percent of Ulster's students. But the numbers are growing. Now that the integrated movement has government financial support, more and more schools should become integrated. When that happens, polls show that 30 to 40 percent of Northern Ireland's parents would consider sending their children to them.[8]

Throughout the years of conflict in Northern Ireland, there have always been countless numbers of people who have tirelessly demonstrated for peace.

Already, Alan Smith, of the Northern Ireland Council for Integrated Education, claims that the schools are "creating a significant shift in the life of Northern Ireland."9

HOPE FOR THE FUTURE

It remains to be seen how deep and how long-lasting that "significant shift" will be. But so long as efforts like those discussed in this chapter continue, there is hope that peace will eventually come to Northern Ireland. Despite the long history of hate, despite the tribal loyalties, and despite the continuing terrorism—there is hope.

But before that hope can become a reality, the politicians will have to face the very real political problems that confront the province. Most of all, they must somehow come together and establish some sort of government for Ulster.

9

OBSTACLES TO
THE FUTURE

Ultimately, there are only three options for the political future of Northern Ireland:

- It will remain a province of the United Kingdom.

- It will be reunited with the rest of Ireland.

- It will become an independent state.

Each of these options is legally possible. Given the support of both the Protestant and Catholic communities, any one of them might turn out to be the key to lasting peace. Whichever option is finally chosen, it will have to be carried out under conditions acceptable to both communities. If not, it will simply set the stage for new Troubles in the future.

Unfortunately, each of the possible options has the angry opposition of a major segment of either the Protestant community or the Catholic community. The nationalists, of course, refuse to accept even the possibility of staying within the United Kingdom. The unionists are just as bitterly opposed to ever joining the rest of Ireland. And the great majority of *both* communities oppose the idea of an independent Ulster.

In each case, the most bitter opponents of the proposed solutions are the most determined and violent elements of the community. They are the ones who make up the IRA on the one hand, and the UDA and UVF on the other. As these elements have already shown, they are more than powerful enough to scuttle any political settlement they oppose—at least as long as they have the passive support of a large segment of their own community.

If a political solution is ever to be found, the people of Ulster and the politicians who represent them are going to have to bypass the extremists and the terrorists. They are going to have to decide to cooperate with each other, at least long enough to find some form of government that both communities can live with and build a future upon.

There is some reason to hope that the people, at least, are beginning to realize the need for cooperation. A 1988 poll showed that a surprising 70 percent of the people of Northern Ireland favor some form of power sharing.[1] But in order for any system of power sharing to be worked out, Northern Ireland's politicians must be willing to compromise. And, unfortunately, compromise has always been the hardest of all things for Ulster's politicians to achieve.

Early in 1989, it was revealed that some Unionist leaders had met secretly with some nationalist leaders in a hotel in West Germany. When word of the meeting got out, the politicians reacted as though they had been caught doing something indecent. They called off plans for further talks, hotly denying that they reached any kind of a compromise with each other.[2]

In most Western countries, political compromise is considered a desirable thing. It is a way to make a democratic society work. But not in Northern Ireland. There, as Sister Anna points out, " 'Compromise' is considered a bad word."3 Ask the politicians who met in Germany. Or ask Michael Collins. One of the most skilled and ruthless of the early leaders of the IRA, Collins was the one who negotiated the treaty that ended the Anglo-Irish War. By doing so, he laid the foundations for the Irish Free State. And yet, when he signed that historic treaty, he announced that he was also signing his own death warrant.4 Less than a year later, he was gunned down from ambush.

It isn't clear whether Collins was murdered for his support of the Anglo-Irish treaty or for some other reason. But it is reasonable to think that the treaty may have cost him his life. The forces opposed to any compromise in Ireland have always been strong and violent. It is not surprising that today's politicians in Ulster fear that supporting any kind of compromise may mean throwing away their careers, if not their lives.

This reluctance—even fear—to compromise makes the search for a political solution to Northern Ireland's problems extremely difficult. And yet *some* solution must eventually be found. *Some* option must eventually be taken.

The tragedy of Northern Ireland is that so many people on both sides have closed their minds to compromise. In a sense, they have closed their minds to the possibility of peace. The only possibility they recognize now is victory. They feel that to compromise would be to betray the past that is still alive in Ireland.

For these Catholics, compromise would mean betraying Wolfe Tone, Father Murphy, and all the victims of the dreaded Oliver Cromwell. For these Protestants, it would mean betraying William of Orange and the martyrs of Portadown and Wexford. For all of them, it would mean the betrayal of the many ancestors and comrades who have already sacrificed their lives for the cause—whether that cause was a Catholic Ireland or a Protestant Ulster.

To compromise now, for these people, would be like saying that all that pain, devotion, and suffering were unnecessary. After all, what has changed? If compromise is possible now, it was possible before. And, unfortunately for the future of Northern Ireland, too many people on both sides of the peace lines are not yet ready to face that one simple—and terrible—fact.

SOURCE NOTES

CHAPTER ONE

1. Rose, Richard. *Governing Without Consensus* (London: Faber, 1971), p. 74.

2. *Encyclopaedia Britannica* (Chicago: Encyclopaedia Britannica, 1985), vol. 24, p. 132.

3. *The World Almanac and Book of Facts 1988* (New York: World Almanac, 1987), p. 537.

4. "Ancestry and Language in the United States," *Current Populations Reports* (Washington, DC: U.S. Government Printing Office, 1982).

5. Phillips, Andrew. "An Unlikely Terrorist," *Maclean's*, September 26, 1988, p. 30.

6. Bierman, John. "A Land of Hate," *Maclean's*, September 26, 1988, p. 24.

7. Interview on ABC-TV's "Nightline," 1988.

8. Phillips, p. 26.

9. "Liberties Fall Victim to Latest IRA Surge," *U.S. News & World Report*, November 7, 1988, p. 47.

10. Barich, Bill. "Ulster Spring," *The New Yorker*, November 21, 1988, pp. 114–115.

11. The first of these estimates was reported by J. D. Reed (and others) in "Terror in the Cemetery," *Time*, March 28, 1988, p. 34; the second in Fay Willey and Donna Foote's "The

Unquiet Graves of Belfast," *Newsweek*, March 28, 1988, p. 41.

12. This description of the events at Milltown Cemetery on March 16, 1988, is based on television news footage, as well as on published accounts, including Reed, and Willey and Foote, above, and Thomas Flanagan's "Poised Between Slaughters," *Time*, April 4, 1988, p. 32.

13. Like the description of the events at Milltown Cemetery, this account is based both on television footage and on published accounts, particularly Flanagan (above), and "Notes and Comment," *The New Yorker*, April 11, 1988, p. 29.

14. NINS (Northern Ireland News Service) Report, April 18, 1989.

15. Quoted in "Notes and Comment" (above), p. 30.

CHAPTER TWO

1. Kee, Robert. *Ireland: A History* (Boston: Little, Brown, 1982), p. 25.

2. Ibid., p. 29.

3. Sanderson, Edgar, and others. *History and Its Makers* (New York: E.R. Du Mont, 1899), vol. I, pp. 370–371.

4. O'Brien, Maire, and Conor Cruise O'Brien. *The Story of Ireland* (New York: Viking Press, 1972), p. 47.

5. Ibid., p. 32.

6. Kee, p. 58.

7. O'Ballance, Edgar. *Terror in Ireland* (Novato, CA: Presidio Press, 1981), p. 5.

8. The O'Briens, p. 62.

9. Kee, pp. 41–42.

10. Testimony of Elizabeth Prize, given before British Royal Commissioners investigating the uprising of 1641. Quoted in Kee, p. 43.

11. From a letter of Oliver Cromwell to the speaker of the British Parliament, quoted in Charles Carlton's *Bigotry and Blood: Documents on the Ulster Troubles* (Chicago: Nelson-Hall, 1977), p. 28.

12. The O'Briens, pp. 68–69.

13. This is the phrase used in the initiation oath of the first Orange Lodge, founded in 1795. Quoted in Andrew Boyd's *Holy War in Belfast* (New York: Grove Press, 1969), p. 7.

14. Kee, p. 10.

15. O'Ballance, p. 10.

16. Shivers, Lynne, and David Bowman, S.J. *More Than the Troubles* (Philadelphia: New Society Publishers, 1984), p. 103.

17. Quoted in Thomas J. O'Hanlon's *The Irish* (New York: Harper and Row, 1975), p. 70.

18. For more about Henry Grattan, see Stephen Gwynn's *Henry Grattan and His Times* (Westport, CT: Greenwood Press, 1971).

19. "The Constitution of the United Irishmen," as reprinted in Carlton, p. 46.

20. Ibid., page 46.

21. MacEoin, Gary. *Northern Ireland: Captive of History* (New York: Holt, Rinehart and Winston, 1974), p. 125.

22. Kee, p. 64.

23. The French-inspired Wexford rebellion was the subject of an intriguing BBC (British Broadcasting Corporation) television documentary, "Spark of Revolution," in 1989.

24. "Croppies Lie Down," reprinted in *Songs of Irish Rebellion*, George Zimmerman, ed. (Hatboro, PA: Folklore Associates, 1967), pp. 308–309.

25. "Father Murphy of the County of Wexford." Ibid., pp. 290–291.

26. For more about Wolfe Tone, see Frank MacDermot's *Theobald Wolfe Tone and His Times* (Tralee, Ireland: Anvil Books, 1980).

27. Quoted in Kee, p. 69.

28. NINS Report, July 13, 1989.

29. MacEoin, p. 122.

CHAPTER THREE

1. For more about Daniel O'Connell, see Angus D. Macintyre's *The Liberator: Daniel O'Connell and the Irish Party* (New York: Macmillan, 1965).

2. O'Ballance, p. 14.

3. "Transactions of the Central Relief Committee of the Society of Friends during the Famine in Ireland in 1847" (Dublin: Hodges and Smith, 1852), p. 163. (Reprinted in Carlton's *Bigotry and Blood*.)

4. For an excellent short account of the suffering in Ireland

during the Great Famine and the British response to it, see Kee, pp. 77–101. For a more detailed account of the famine, see Cecil Woodham-Smith's *The Great Hunger*. (London: Hamish Hamilton, 1962).

5. Shivers, Lynne, and David Bowman. *More Than the Troubles* (Philadelphia: New Society Publishers, 1984), p. 105.

6. Chancellor of the Exchequer Charles Wood, quoted in Kee, p. 87.

7. Quoted in Kee, p. 86.

8. O'Hanlon, p. 117.

9. Kee, p. 94.

10. For more on the Young Ireland movement, see Denis Gwynn's *Young Ireland and 1848* (Cork, Ireland: Cork University Press, 1949).

11. *History and Its Makers*, vol. II, p. 427.

12. Ibid., p. 432.

13. For a detailed account of the Easter uprising, see Max Caulfield's *The Easter Rebellion* (London: Frederick Muller, 1964).

14. O'Ballance, p. 29.

15. *Northern Ireland.* An information booklet published by the Central Office of Information, London 1988, p. 2.

16. Kee, p. 182.

17. *Northern Ireland*, p. 3.

18. MacEoin, p. 169.

19. O'Ballance, p. 35.

20. MacEoin, p. 172.

21. Ibid., p. 55.

22. *Encyclopaedia Britannica*, vol. 24, p. 137.

23. MacEoin, p. 54.

CHAPTER FOUR

1. The O'Briens, p. 169.

2. Ibid.

3. Shivers and Bowman, p. 117.

4. Ibid.

5. This famous speech is quoted in Terence O'Neill's own book, *Ulster at the Crossroads* (London: Faber and Faber, 1969), pp. 140–146.

6. Shivers and Bowman, p. 117.

7. MacEoin, p. 226.

8. O'Ballance, p. 116.

9. Quoted in *Chronicle of the 20th Century* (Mount Kisco, NY: Chronicle Publications, 1987), p. 999.

10. *Northern Ireland: Points at Issue,* a publication of the Foreign and Commonwealth Office, London, January 1988, pp. 7–12.

11. MacEoin, p. 235.

12. Ibid., p. 234.

13. Ibid., p. 225.

14. Shivers and Bowman, p. 120.

15. MacEoin, p. 257.

16. *Chronicle*, p. 1043.

17. O'Ballance, p. 167.

18. *Northern Ireland.* An information booklet published by the Central Office of Information, London, 1988, p. 5.

19. MacEoin, pp. 261–262.

20. NINS Report, June 22, 1989.

21. *Northern Ireland: A Brief Survey.* A reference booklet published by the Central Office of Information, London, 1988, p. 8.

22. Ibid., p. 9.

23. This is the claim of Des O'Malley, a former cabinet minister and current head of the Progressive Democrats in the Republic. NINS Report, June 12, 1989.

24. The O'Briens, p. 167.

25. Interview by the author.

26. *Northern Ireland: Points at Issue*, p. 21.

27. NINS Report, May 9, 1989.

28. The then British secretary of state for Ulster, Tom King, quoted in a NINS Report, May 24, 1989.

CHAPTER FIVE

1. *Fodor's Ireland 1988* (New York: Fodor's Travel Publications, 1987), p. 293.

2. According to *The Development of a City—Belfast,* a 1986 publication of the Northern Ireland Department of the Environment.

3. O'Ballance, p. 15.
4. Barich, p. 101.
5. Ibid., p. 112.
6. Interview by the author, March 17, 1989.
7. *Northern Ireland: A Brief Survey*, p. 17.
8. *Northern Ireland*, pp. 17–18.
9. NINS Report, May 2, 1989.
10. NINS Report, December 22, 1988.
11. These figures are computed from those given in *Northern Ireland*, p. 1 and pp. 16–17.
12. NINS Report, February 7, 1988.
13. NINS Report, June 22, 1989.
14. NINS Report, July 31, 1989.
15. NINS Report, June 21, 1989.
16. Barich, p. 110.
17. NINS Report, May 10, 1989.
18. *Northern Ireland*, p. 15.
19. Ibid., p. 16.

CHAPTER SIX

1. NINS Report, January 3, 1988.
2. This is a paraphrase of an anonymous remark quoted by MacEoin, p. 35.
3. Interview by the author, March 14, 1989.
4. Quoted in "IRA Hopes Guerrilla Tactics Will Hit Home with Britons," by Eldon Knoche, in the *Milwaukee Sentinel*, September 22, 1988, p. 12.
5. This is the opinion of many observers, including Sister Anna and Caroline Cracraft of the British Consulate-General.
6. Shivers and Bowman, p. 3.
7. "Liberties Fall Victim to the Latest IRA Surge," p. 47.
8. Rose, p. 534.
9. This true story is told by Sister Anna, an Episcopalian nun, who is one of the leading campaigners for integrated schools in Northern Ireland.
10. "Catholic-Protestant Hostility Paralyzes Belfast's Politics," by Eldon Knoche, in the *Milwaukee Sentinel*, September 21, 1988, p. 9.
11. NINS Special Report by Tom Collins, May 18–19, 1989.
12. MacEoin, p. 32.

CHAPTER SEVEN

1. British government figures, quoted in a NINS Report, April 17, 1989.

2. For those interested in the subject of terrorism, see Michael Kronenwetter's *War on Terrorism* (Englewood Cliffs, NJ: Messner, 1989).

3. MacEoin, p. 44.

4. Quoted by John Newhouse, in "A Freemasonry of Terrorism," *The New Yorker*, July 8, 1985, p. 61.

5. Barich, p. 108.

6. NINS Report, April 11, 1989.

7. NINS Report, April 13, 1989.

8. NINS Report, March 17, 1989.

9. Bilski, Andrew, and others. "The Violent Majority," *Maclean's*, September 26, 1988, p. 33.

10. *Northern Ireland Unscrambler*, a reference sheet published by the Northern Ireland News Service, 1988.

11. *Northern Ireland: Points at Issue*. A publication of the Foreign and Commonwealth Office, London, 1988, p. 13–21.

12. Barich, p. 104.

13. Delaney, Mary Murray. *Of Irish Ways* (New York: Kilkenny Press, 1973), p. 305.

14. Barich, p. 122.

15. NINS Report, July 26, 1989.

16. "An Unlikely Terrorist," p. 28.

17. Bilski, p. 33.

18. "The Unquiet Graves of Belfast," p. 41.

19. NINS Report, April 17, 1989.

20. NINS Report, February 18, 1989.

21. NINS Report, February 9, 1989.

22. NINS Report, April 17, 1989.

23. Bilski, p. 33.

24. "A Shadow Government," *Newsweek*, September 12, 1988, p. 38.

25. Reports of the scandal were international. Some of the details here were originally released by Independent Television News and reported in a NINS Special Report by Tom Collins, May 4, 1989.

26. For an interesting article on the network of international

terrorism, see John Newhouse's "A Freemasonry of Terrorism," in *The New Yorker*, July 8, 1985.

27. NINS Report, April 14, 1989.

28. *Northern Ireland: Points at Issue*, pp. 11–12.

29. NINS Report, March 13, 1989.

30. *Amnesty International Report 1988* (London: Amnesty International Publications, 1988), p. 222.

31. "Liberties Fall Victim to the Latest IRA Surge," p. 47.

32. *Amnesty International Report 1988*, p. 221.

33. Ibid.

34. NINS Report, December 28, 1988.

35. Quoted in "A Report from the Land of the Troubles," by Robert O'Connor, *America*, May 21, 1988, p. 527.

36. NINS Report, April 5, 1989.

37. National Public Radio news report, November 28, 1988.

38. "Sunday Today," NBC Television, 1989.

39. NINS Report, March 13, 1989.

40. "Green and Unpleasant Land," *The New Republic*, April 11, 1988, p. 8.

CHAPTER EIGHT

1. See *Fair Employment in Northern Ireland*, a white paper published by Her Majesty's Stationery Office, London, in May 1988.

2. Detailed and up-to-date information about the International Fund for Ireland can be obtained in its latest annual report, available through both British and Irish embassies and consulates in the United States.

3. "Two Peace Prizes from Oslo," *Time*, October 24, 1977, p. 54.

4. "Two Women of Ulster," *Newsweek*, October 24, 1977, p. 61.

5. See *Peace and Reconciliation Projects in Ireland*. A directory edited by Ian M. Ellis. (Belfast and Dublin: Co-operation North, 1984).

6. Interview by the author.

7. This account of All Children Together and the birth of Lagan College is based largely on the author's interview with Sister Anna.

8. "Generating New Hope," *Newsweek*, December 5, 1988, p. 90.
9. Ibid., p. 91.

CHAPTER NINE

1. "Liberties Fall Victim to the Latest IRA Surge," p. 47.
2. NINS Report, February 3, 1989.
3. Interview by the author, March 14, 1989.
4. O'Ballance, p. 40.

FOR FURTHER READING

For a continuous flow of up-to-date information about events in Northern Ireland, libraries, schools, and even individuals can subscribe to the NewsBreaks of the Northern Ireland News Service, Box 57, Albany, New York 12211. NINS is about as objective a source of information about what is actually happening in Northern Ireland as is currently available. Its News-Breaks, which come out roughly once or twice a week, have been invaluable to me in writing this book.

BOOKS OF INTEREST

For information on the history of Ireland as a whole and Ulster in particular:

Kee, Robert. *Ireland: A History.* Boston: Little, Brown, 1982.

MacEoin, Gary. *Northern Ireland: Captive of History.* New York: Holt, Rinehart and Winston, 1974.

McCaffrey, Lawrence J. *Ireland: From Colony to Nation.* Englewood Cliffs, NJ: Prentice Hall, 1979.

O'Ballance, Edgar. *Terror in Ireland.* Novato, CA: Presidio Press, 1981.

O'Brien, Maire, and Conor Cruise O'Brien. *The Story of Ireland.* New York: Viking Press, 1972.

For revealing personal looks at what it is like to live in the midst of, and in some cases take part in, the struggle in Ulster:

Belfrage, Sally. *Living with War: A Belfast Year.* New York: Elisabeth Sifton Books/Viking, 1988.

Holland, Jack. *Too Long a Sacrifice: Life and Death in Northern Ireland Since 1969.* New York: Dodd, 1981.

For examinations of the IRA, from various points of view:

Bell, J. Bowyer. *The Secret Army: The IRA, 1916–1979.* Revised. Cambridge, MA: MIT Press, 1971.

Brown, Richard Howard. *I Am of Ireland.* New York: Harper and Row, 1974.

McGuire, Maria. *To Take Arms: My Year with the Provisionals.* New York: Viking Press, 1973.

Other books of special interest:

Boyd, Andrew. *Holy War in Belfast.* New York: Grove Press, 1972.

Carlton, Charles. *Bigotry and Blood: Documents on the Ulster Troubles.* Chicago: Nelson-Hall, 1977.

Chartres, John, Bert Henshaw, and Michael Dewar. *Northern Ireland Scrapbook.* London: Arms and Armour Press, 1986.

Rose, Richard. *Governing Without Consensus: An Irish Perspective.* London: Faber, 1971.

Shivers, Lynne, and David Bowman. *More Than the Troubles.* Philadelphia: New Society Publishers, 1984.

MAGAZINE ARTICLES

Barich, Bill. "Ulster Spring," *The New Yorker,* November 21, 1988.

Bierman, John. "A Land of Hate," *Maclean's,* September 26, 1988.

Bilski, Andrew, and others. "The Violent Majority," *Maclean's*,
   September 26, 1988.
Flanagan, Thomas. "Poised Between Slaughters," *Time*, April
   4, 1988.
"Green and Unpleasant Land," *The New Republic*, April 11,
   1988.
Phillips, Andrew. "An Unlikely Terrorist," *Maclean's*, Septem-
   ber 26, 1988.

INDEX

ABOUT THE AUTHOR

Michael Kronenwetter is a freelance writer who writes about contemporary issues. His other books for Franklin Watts include *Are You a Liberal? Are You a Conservative?*; *Free Press v. Fair Trial: Television and Other Media in the Courtroom*; *Capitalism vs. Socialism: Economic Policies of the U.S. and U.S.S.R.*; *Journalism Ethics*; *The Military Power of the President*; *Politics and the Press*; and *Taking a Stand Against Human Rights Abuses*.

Mr. Kronenwetter lives in Wisconsin.